P 43
94
25-76

YONDER

YONDER

Life on the Far Side of Change

JIM W. CORDER

The University of Georgia Press

Athens and London

© 1992 by Jim W. Corder
Published by the University of Georgia Press
Athens, Georgia 30602

Designed by Sandra Strother Hudson
The paper in this book meets the guidelines
for permanence and durability of the Committee on
Production Guidelines for Book Longevity
of the Council on Library Resources.

Printed in the United States of America
96 95 94 93 92 C 5 4 3 2 1

Library of Congress Cataloging in Publication Data

Corder, Jim W. (Jim Wayne), 1929–
Yonder : life on the far side of change / Jim W. Corder.
      p.   cm.
    ISBN 0-8203-1419-6 (alk. paper)
1. Corder, Jim W. (Jim Wayne), 1929–   .   2. Social change.
          3. Educators—Texas—Biography.
  4. Authors, American—20th century—Biography.   I. Title.
CT275.C7813A3   1992
976.4'06'092—dc20
[B]
                                                      91-33931
                                                        CIP

British Library Cataloging in Publication Data available

FOR ROBERTA

Contents

Preface *ix*

BEGINNING

1. Restaurant Nora *3*

2. The Search for the Perfect Peanut *6*

AFTER

3. After *17*

4. Cast of Characters *25*

5. After *27*

6. Which Text Do We Use in This Course? *28*

7. If I Don't Know What Time It Is,
   Do I Know Who I Am? *31*

8. Dislocation *36*

9. The Farm Is Gone *38*

10. The Personnel Office *44*

11. Can I Get a Witness? *52*

12. Show and Tell *56*

13. What Happens Then? *58*

14. And Then What Happens? *59*

LATER

15. Counting the Losses *63*

16. Losing the Count *75*

17. The Snapshots I Have and the Snapshots I Don't Have *77*

18. Already a Little Fuzzy Around the Edges   *87*

19. Bob Coluci Died Last Week, and I'm Still Counting   *96*

20. I Proposed a New Geography Course, but the
    Curriculum Committee Turned It Down   *123*

21. The Ache for Home   *149*

22. When Rhetorics Collide   *162*

23. Speak, Memory   *174*

24. Disappearing   *178*

25. I Am the Twentieth Century   *180*

26. The Lux Radio Theater   *185*

YONDER

27. Jackleg Carpentry   *201*

28. Domestic Privacies   *204*

29. Long Walks   *206*

30. Hiding   *208*

31. To the Jayton Cemetery   *213*

32. Gateway   *221*

Sources and Acknowledgments   *227*

Preface

If this is a memoir or an autobiography, I'll be surprised. Some historian, say, and my mother, were she still here, might testify that I have no occasion to write a memoir or autobiography; the historian, perhaps, because I am not notable and have not been where the momentous occurs, my mother, perhaps, because if I've called attention to myself, I ought to be ashamed and to hush. I don't know how to respond to what my mother might have said, but the historian would be wrong: every one of us is notable and lives among momentous events. Every one of us occasions a book—or a library—because each of us is unique, and because each of us is not unique.

The truth, I'm inclined to think, does not incarnate itself in us. To say that it does would be to say that the truth exists prior to ourselves and without our meddling. Such truth as we're likely to claim is in us, I expect, and with us, and rises from us, sometimes becoming public, sometimes remaining private. Some things remain private with me; other things—far more—wouldn't matter much to anyone else. I do, however, tell about some events, circumstances, and conditions of my life.

But I don't much think that makes this a memoir or an autobiography. I do commence and end with myself, and in between I check regularly with myself to be sure that I'm still there. I believe in the significance of regular time and ordinary life, and mine is the one I know, or mostly know. But after all, I don't think that I am subject, object, and occasion for what follows. In that, I'd generally agree with what my mother might have said.

I called this book *Yonder* for a variety of reasons. I like the sound of the word. I like the idea of looking far, looking yonder, whether ahead, behind, upward, downward, or on the bias. Sometimes, yonder, we find ourselves in places where the private and the public are not separate, where each informs and reenacts the other.

So, I think, it has been with me. I have been in change, as we all have, sometimes minor, sometimes major, and I have been trying to look far in this direction, then that, then yonder, hoping I might see what life is like on the far side of change. What happens to our culture, I think, usually happens to us; what happens to us usually happens to our culture. The culture has known exodus, *volkswanderung*, and migration; we have left the farm for the city, have left our homes for elsewhere. The culture has known war and holocaust; we have experienced personal disaster and loss. The great and the small are in each other, I think, and each tells about the other. When change comes, whether to a culture or to one of us, it jars and threatens, sometimes only a little, sometimes almost more than we can bear. After dislocation, in the time and distance after change, I think I am not alone in being pulled both by what was and won't go away, by what is and will remain. I wanted this to be an exploration of what happens to us after *any* great change. I'm reckoning that both individuals and societies, after any great change, experience a sense of loss, an ensuing nostalgia, a failure of memory, and a profound confusion of languages and values. I wanted the book to be a scholarly sort of work written in a personal sort of way. As deliberately as I could, I made it personal, but I don't much think it's ever just personal. I wanted change to be known as immediate and personal; I wanted history to be present, to hurt. I hoped to see what life is like on the far side of change. I hoped I might see what there is in my circumstances that would let me lift the personal up to public scrutiny, bring the public in to private scrutiny.

I want to thank Malcolm Call and Stanley Lindberg for the uncommon kindness, understanding, and thoroughness of their assistance and support in the preparation of the manuscript. I am also grateful to Sam Pickering for his insight and advice, and to Claudia Knott, Maura Cuny, and Angela Huber, who typed the manuscript. I hope the dedication expresses some of my gratitude for the deliverance that has been given to me.

BEGINNING

Restaurant Nora

Today is Wednesday, June 1, 1988. I am in Murphy's Pub, just off Connecticut Avenue N.W. and across the street from the Sheraton Washington. We were here on Sunday night for dinner and for the music later, and we were here for lunch on Monday. Since, I've made occasion and time to be here on Tuesday morning, and again in the afternoon, on Wednesday morning, and now again in the afternoon, though I should say, for my self's sake, that I've been elsewhere, too.

I've ridden the Metro, though I haven't been brave enough to change lines or swift enough to understand the fare cards, and have accumulated, therefore, a fair number, each with twenty cents remaining. On Sunday we caught the Metro at Woodley Park Zoo, rode down past Dupont Circle and Farragut North, turned east, and got off at Metro Center. From there we walked west on F Street, looped around the Treasury Building, north around the White House by Lafayette Square and back down by the Corcoran, out onto the grass, down by the Vietnam Veterans' Memorial—crowded that Sunday before Memorial Day with grieving relatives and friends, interested bypassers, and professional Vietnam Veterans—and on to say hello to Mr. Lincoln. Then we headed east and finally reached the National Art Gallery and, later, the Air and Space Museum. By the time we finished, glad of rest, we caught a cab and stopped across the street from our hotel at Murphy's Pub.

From fatigue, not from poverty of choice. I read about restaurants and make lists. I read the guides in hotel rooms and convention packets. Sometimes I read the listings in telephone directories. I make lists and wonder about them all. I remembered the American Café from that time before with Cathy. I listed the Ambassador Grill and Bacchus and the Bombay Palace, Café Mozart and the China Inn and Galileo, the Old Ebbitt Grill and

Thai Taste (where we'd have lunch) and Montmartre (another lunch), Le Pavillon and the Ethiopian Messkerem (where we'd have dinner), and Marrakesh, a Moroccan place (another dinner). But that night we came to Murphy's Pub. Turned out well, too: good stew, good corned beef and cabbage, good music by young Kevin Farley.

He sang some modestly satirical contemporary songs ("I'll sing anything / Even 'God Save the King.' / But I just won't sing Bob Dylan") but mostly older Irish songs, and I remembered again how often either the words or the music, somewhere, sometime down the long road from Ireland to Texas, had been transformed into the country music I grew up with, so that songs he sang that I'd never heard sounded nonetheless familiar. And I wondered again whether or not a good folk singer, whose music may be lost in beer talk as dark comes down, might be as much artist as someone who's taped and sanctified; whether or not a good folk singer might make art as good in its way as the sometimes minor canvases that happened to survive and to reach some gallery wall. Anyway, his songs with the guitar were good, the jigs and reels with the fiddle better.

But I've done otherwise than sit in Murphy's Pub, though that would suit me well enough. I walked down Connecticut Avenue to Dupont Circle and found my memory wrong again. I had thought it was just south of the circle, but I came just north of the circle to the office of the National Association for the Education of Young Children, where Cathy worked that time before. I stood across the street and looked at the narrow, three-story building of dark red brick with white trim. Ivy covers more of the wall than it did before. Just off Dupont Circle, at 1724 20th N.W., I found Earthworks, a pipe and tobacco shop, though half the space was given to quainter smoking equipment than burley and briar; and across the way, at 1606 20th N.W., I found Vincenzo, where we had dinner that long time before, still in my mind the best seafood I've ever eaten. I rode to Farragut North and found Garfinkel's pipe and tobacco shop at 1585 I, N.W.

I walked back, and not far off Dupont Circle, at 2132 Florida Avenue N.W., found Restaurant Nora. We had lunch there that other time, and I was glad to see it again. Places change while I'm not watching, even when the time for change is brief, and I find myself uncommonly grateful and relieved, as if a prayer were answered, as if even death were delayed, when a dear place, or a familiar place, or just a place that mattered momentarily, has survived so that I can see it again and try to get the look of it into my head. I didn't go in. I looked and read the menu posted outside and enjoyed thinking about chicken breast with a stuffing of pecans and ham and a sage sauce, about grilled lamb chops in a sesame marinade with ginger sauce.

I looked and read and came away, back to Murphy's Pub. In front of me, on two shelves back of the bar, are peach schnapps, Galliano, Frangelico, crème de almond, sloe gin, Remy Martin cognac, Hennessey cognac, Courvoisier cognac, and, on the higher shelf, crème de menthe, crème de cacao, white crème de cacao, crème de cassis, anisette, and cherry brandy, blackberry brandy, peach brandy, apricot brandy, strawberry brandy. I have wondered if I could come to understand why I was so relieved to find Restaurant Nora still there, could come to understand the lists, the names and places of things, the way they look in my head, the way they look when I see them. I have wondered that they matter and why they matter. Do I only serve myself in foolish ways, needing to know the names and the look of places, things, and people for testimony that the world exists, so that I might imagine for a while longer that I, too, exist? When everything always changes and some things disappear, perhaps in the process I, too, vanish. I have wondered if such things matter. Perhaps I have only perpetuated silly habits from old time.

2

The Search for the Perfect Peanut

To be sure, I have spent time and spirit in searches that were, if not unintelligible, at least wonderfully trivial.

In 1941 I started in junior high school and discovered maps. I came to love them, and have since. I don't have what anyone else would call a map collection. I don't search for rare old maps. I am only a looker and keeper.

The wall of my study upstairs at home is covered with maps, mostly the big foldout maps that come periodically in *National Geographic*. Over my desk is a big map of the United States. On either side are maps of England and Europe and Mexico and the West Indies and the Near East, and another map of the United States without state boundaries. It shows where American Indian tribes mostly lived. Among the maps there is also a big poster, the one my daughter brought from England that shows RAF planes. Behind me, on the other wall, are maps of the New England states and the southeastern states and California and Africa. I lean back and read the names.

I also have maps stacked and folded here, there, and yonder in my office. The atlas of the United States lies on top of books in a shelf close by my desk. It's worn. The cover is still there but is no longer fastened to the book. On another shelf is a group of maps my daughter gave me for Christmas—Caney Creek Wilderness and Ouachita National Forest in Arkansas, the Pecos Wilderness in the Carson and Santa Fe National Forest in New Mexico, the Caddo–Lyndon B. Johnson Grasslands, the whole Santa Fe National Forest, and the Davy Crockett National Forest. Nearby is a pile of maps I accumulated from the American Automobile Association for a trip across Louisiana to Vicksburg, across Mississippi, angling up through Alabama to Chattanooga and on by back roads to Gatlinburg and down onto the Blue Ridge Parkway and up through North Carolina and Virginia to Washington, then back down West Virginia and across Kentucky and down to Memphis and across Arkansas and home. Underneath that group of maps is a large envelope that holds more. They show the way to the Big Bend, on up to El Paso, then up the west side of New Mexico to Durango, Colorado, and Mesa Verde, and back by Santa Fe and home. With them, rolled up and held by a rubber band, are four large county maps. They show King, Dickens, Kent, and Stonewall counties, all in sufficient detail to mark the farm and ranch houses, and all roads, even the two-rut dirt roads that Mindy always enjoyed. Farther down the shelf is a big heavy book that has enlarged maps of all 254 Texas counties. Beside it is a cardboard box with brown and orange stripes; it is filled with maps. On my desk there is a new collection of maps from last summer. They tell the way across Arkansas and part of Tennessee and north across Kentucky and slantwise across Ohio and to Penn State University for a conference and on from there to Boston and on to Concord, New Hampshire, and from there to Portsmouth and to the White Mountains and across the Kancamagus Highway and to Freeport, Maine, and then southward, down across Massachusetts and Connecticut and through New York City and down the New Jersey Turnpike and alongside Philadelphia and across corners of Delaware and Maryland and along by Baltimore and Washington and down through Virginia and North Carolina to Myrtle Beach and then home across South Carolina and Georgia and Alabama and Mississippi and Louisiana. I finger the maps and read the names.

If I became obsessed with maps in the seventh grade, I didn't know it. I expect I thought I was just looking. Perhaps I had not seen many maps before that time. I can't remember. But that year I was in a geography class, and the textbook was big and filled with maps. In those days we had a required study hall during one period. I didn't much like doing my homework in study hall, so I spent the entire period, day after day, week after week, looking at the wonderful maps in my geography book. I wanted to know the names of places.

And more: I wanted to keep the names. I made lists—lists of countries and rivers and mountains and deserts, lists of cities and towns and villages. I still don't know why.

Perhaps I just wanted to know and to keep the name of things.

Perhaps I was feeling a little lost in the big city. We had come from a little town of fewer than 700 souls to a place where 200,000 and more people lived all together in houses on houses, buildings on buildings. (I told my children later that the 700 didn't include Boone Bilberry, that you couldn't count him: the Baptists said he didn't have a soul, and besides, he was often a little fuzzy around the edges and sometimes disappeared altogether. Mr. Bilberry drank a little.) I had been used to familiar places and to empty places, and now, wherever I walked, I couldn't find them.

Maps were soon dear to me, and are still. I realized pretty early that maps are maps, not places. When we make maps or paint pictures or write, we're trying to render one kind of experience through another kind of experience, territories and people through pictures, lives through words.

The pictures and the words, then, are going to be imperfect, but they hold and last a while and let us send small messages back and forth. I came to cherish maps. Maps will hold awhile as things change, places change, and we go on. They are treasures, though imperfect, even if the geographies they show are sometimes far away. I wanted to know and to keep the names.

And I can't claim that my aspirations were later much elevated.

I've spent more than a little time all these years looking for reminders of what I thought I saw, for authentication of what I thought I saw, for the remainder of things I saw part of, for all of what I missed. In my mind, or wherever such things are kept, are images—some clear, some cloudy—of marvelous airplanes that flew back when I was twelve or fifteen and older brothers were fighting World War II. The planes had striking names—Hurricane, Defiant, Avenger, Mustang, Corsair, Mosquito, Beaufighter, Thunderbolt, and on. I still sketch a fair Spitfire when I'm in committee meetings, and a passable Warhawk. But until I checked out Peter Bowers's *Forgotten Fighters and Experimental Aircraft*, I had quite forgotten one plane that I thought was especially thrilling to look at so long ago. There it was, on page 92, the Grumman XP-50, a two-engine fighter that never made it into production.

But it didn't disappear forever. I found it again. Les Daniels's book *Comix: A History of Comic Books in America*, has a six-page sample spread from the old comic book "Black Hawk" that began publication in 1944, and sure enough, in the last panel, having triumphed again over enemies of the Allies, the seven fierce heroes fly off in their Grumman XP-50s.

I found both books at the main public library downtown. I go there maybe forty-five or forty-six Saturdays of the fifty-two a year gives to follow the uncertain trail of a junk-filled mind, and I take great pleasure in trivial joys. When I occasionally feel a need to justify myself, I think of it all as isometric exercises for the brain.

I fell into the habit of going to the public library when my children were young and I took them there. When I'm working or studying, I go to the university library. I haven't used it up. It supports my work well enough, but it doesn't always feed my fancy, doesn't always yield what I want when I want to read and look for fun. I've just about used up the university holdings in contemporary poetry—I'm a faithful but slapdash reader. At first, then, I depended on the public library for more new poetry. There are 106 shelves of American poetry there, or about 370 feet, and I've still got a way to go.

Then, especially in the last two or three years, I began to branch out. First it was to books about Texas. I didn't want regular old history books; I wanted oddities, backroads, county stories, especially from that sketch of Texas east of I-35 and north of I-20; and in the 40 shelves (or some 140 feet) that I haunt (the 976.4 series and over in 917, too) I have found books on Texas forts and trails that I enjoy, including Ray Miller's series, the *Eyes of Texas Travel Guides*.

Then it was over to the fine arts section, where there are some 750 shelves (about 2,600 feet) holding diverse visual arts and crafts. I've only just begun there. I've just about looked the pictures off the pages in Edwin Wade's *The Arts of the North American Indian* and Patricia Broder's *The American West: The Modern Vision* and Michael Frary's *Impressions of the Texas Panhandle*. I've admired Gail Levin's *Hopper's Places*—a study of Edward Hopper's paintings against photographs of the places he painted—and the lessons in composition would benefit my freshman writing students. I've found books about wine labels and book markers and California orange crate labels, and books about comic strips that let me catch up on Tarzan and Wonder Woman. Reitberger and Fuchs's *Comics: Anatomy of a Mass Medium*, reminded me of the Phantom, a hero I never saw enough of when I was young. Maurice Horn's *Comics of the American West* showed me Rick O'Shay and Hipshot Percussion again.

On down in the fine arts section there are about 100 shelves (around 350 feet) of books on the movies, and I've found John Stanley's *Creature Features Movie Guide* and Jenni Calder's *There Must Be a Lone Ranger*, and books on horror and science fiction movies. In Alan Barbour's *A Thousand and One Delights* (about escapist movies, mostly of the 1940s) I found Claude Rains in *The Phantom of the Opera* and Linda Stirling of *The Tiger Woman* and eleven pages of photographs of Maria Montez in various roles. I see now that she ain't all that much to look at, but when I saw her in *Gypsy Wildcat* in 1944, when I was fourteen, I thought she was really something. Barbour's *The Thrill of It All* (on B westerns) showed me Tom Mix and Buck Jones and Ken Maynard again, and Hoot Gibson and the Three Mesquiteers and Hopalong Cassidy. All this time, I remembered that his shirt and pants were solid black, but a still closeup shows that the pants are a dark stripe. Memory is usually wrong one way or another, one place or time or another. Barbour's *Days of Thrills and Adventures* (on serials) was best of all in this section. I found Buster Crabbe in *Flash Gordon*, and, right there on page 38, a still photo showing Zorro's first entrance in *Zorro Rides Again*. God, he's wonderful. I was doing a pretty good business drawing pictures of Zorro for my third-grade friends until the teacher, Miss Kinney, caught me. It was a tragic moment for me, for I loved her deeply, if not too wildly, from afar and could not easily survive her rebuke.

And then there are airplane books, 33 shelves in three locations, or some 115 feet of books. Wonderful pictures and wonderful details: the nutty marvels in Bowers's *Unconventional Aircraft*, the trim little Curtis Goshawk in Taylor's *Warplanes of the World, 1918–1939*, the lovely little Boeing P-12 in Munson's *Warplanes of Yesteryear*, the wonderful little Gloster Gladiator in Green and Swanborough's *RAF Fighters*. On page 60 in Gunston's *An Illustrated Guide to Allied Fighters of World War II* was the best of all, that other beautiful airplane I had completely forgotten, the Westland Whirlwind, with its daring high tail, slender fuselage, and two huge underslung engines. It doesn't get any better.

Lately, I've checked out Yann Lovelock's *The Vegetable Book*, and rechecked it. A splendid book; it tells the history of vegetables and where they struggled to cease being weeds and to become what we eat. I don't know where the search will go from here, but I do know that it probably won't end. The ritual of the search, the ritual of being there, in the downtown public library that echoes with books and my children, is too pleasurable for me to refrain. I find my treasures and check them out, usually on the lower level that gives directly onto the stores and shops of the Tandy Center. I go up through Dillard's, check the fashions that I can't or won't achieve, and ease on over a block to Billy Miner's Saloon. Linda, who's pretty and pleasant and busy, brings me a Bloody Mary. I've ordered one maybe seventy-two times in a row. I think she has decided that it's what I want. Then, books in my bag on the stool beside me, I commence to hunt for the perfect peanut among the baskets they keep on the bar at Billy Miner's. The search is about as successful as my others.

I have looked for names and have sometimes made lists, have looked for names and people and places and things, sometimes just curious, sometimes hoping to find myself, others, places, things. I have failed. I have looked here, there, yonder, but not everywhere. I don't know how to look everywhere. When you look everywhere, look back or out or sideways or in or out or up, wherever that is, you come at last, from any direction, to the place of which there is no knowledge, of which there can be no knowledge, come to that place but not into it, come only to abut it. I have looked, hoping to find myself, others, places, things.

But I'm not there, nor are others, and the places where we were and the things we knew aren't there. It's a search for what is not, for the thing that never happened, for the place that never was. I'm looking for my memory, not for whoever, whatever was. But that doesn't mean that there is no reason to look, for I am there, too, and the others are, and the places are, and there are always reasons to look, to get situated to see. We ache for home even if it never was; we always know better and don't, and love people or places or times or things — or don't love them — even if they never were, even if they were. Does nostalgia, I wonder, seize us all the more sadly and immediately after great change, amid rapid change, when the new rushes at us far sooner than we can comprehend? Even manna was not enough in the wilderness, and the people fondly remembered Egypt, fondly remembered the fish they ate there, and the cucumbers and the melons and the leeks and the onions and the garlic.

After the Bloody Mary I have a glass of bad but cold white wine and continue searching for the perfect peanut.

At first, I looked casually and contented myself with whatever one handful of peanuts from the closest basket yielded. Early in my search, too, I looked especially for the peanut that was likely to hold three nuts. Soon, I realized that the peanut with two usually gave plumper, better nuts than the peanut with three, which were often smaller and altogether unrewarding. Soon, too, I gave up grabbing a casual handful. I put a napkin folded in fourths on the bar, pulled the nearest basket close, and studied, poking here and there to find the likeliest peanuts, then lined them up on my napkin in what seemed the most promising order, the best saved for last. Finding the right peanut takes time, I guess, and sometimes the search, though unsuccessful, requires a second glass of wine. More recently, I've not been able to content myself with the one basket nearest me. I finger it, to be sure, then slide a farther basket close to check it out. I don't know how much longer I can go on.

The search is not easy, and it comes with dark thoughts. The perfect peanut may not be at Billy Miner's Saloon, now or ever. It may be there on Tuesday or Friday, or it may turn up after I leave on Saturday. And what if it was there before? What if I saw it, took it from the basket, turned it, fingered it, studied it, cracked it, shelled it, and didn't recognize it?

AFTER

3

After

I look for names and try to remember them, and for faces and scenes and things and places; most, I'd guess, are of minor interest or none to others, but not all, and surely not trivial to me. Even when we confess a certain triviality in our interests, I expect we have secret places where we do not mean our confessions; quiet places where, reckoning that much of what happens to any one of us happens in some way to all or most of us, we can suppose that what looks trivial is after all momentous to us, and may be at least on the feathery fringes at the edge of the publicly momentous.

So: it's not surprising to look for names and faces and scenes and things and places and to hope for faithful memory of them. When you keep falling into history, you keep trying to see and hold on. "Often you / Would explore these photographs," Jon Anderson writes, "These memories, in sepia, of another life"; but sometimes it doesn't work, for they are only "the particular fragments / Of an always shattered past." Still, I reason that if I keep looking, someday I might see. And remember. And believe. "The photographs of the summer trip," Billy Collins says in "Strange Lands,"

> are spread
> across the table now like little mirrors
> reflecting our place in European history.

> They are the booty of travel, bordered and colorful,
> split seconds that we pass to friends after dinner
> one by one to make them believe we really found some sweet
> elsewhere, away from here.

Someday, I might even see the world I already know, and then know it again.

I might someday see what I think I know, what I hear about

but don't know, what I've never imagined. People, places, things, events seem to exist. I imagine that I own versions of some, to be sure, but they belong to themselves, not to me alone as their interpreter. I try to catch them. They escape me, but I can learn a little more if I look more carefully. At the far side of the cemetery just outside of Spur, Texas, there is the grave of a little boy, dead at six in 1935. The marker for his grave was made poorly of rough cement. His marbles are embedded in it. I have looked and thought and asked and searched to know him. He slips away from me. I guess how he bent and thumbed his taw. My grandfather's farmhouse burned down about a year after he died some while ago. It was a lonely place, I thought, though dear, on a rise above the highway, up past the railroad trestle. I go there sometimes, though the land belongs to someone else now, and walk and look and try to get myself situated with the sun as he was so that I can see what he saw in the blue distance across the fields, hear, as he heard, the creaking music of the windmill down the way. He slips away, too. He was real before I was, but he loaned me his text, which I keep trying to read.

When Harold Bloom, for example, observes that "there are no texts, but only interpretations," I shake, fearing for my own existence, for the narrative I've made disappears, too, before the thought. Texts—of people and places and things and events and novels and poems and critical essays and meditations and songs and sermons and letters and whatever—seem to exist. Bloom nevertheless seems undeniable when he remarks that "I only know a text, any text, because I know a reading of it, someone else's reading, my own reading, a composite reading," or when he says that in our reading "there is always and only bias, inclination, pre-judgment, swerve." But texts seem to exist, though we may always misread them, reinventing them as we work our way toward ourselves. To be sure, we make our own text of the text we read or hear or watch, but that other text seems to exist. As we read or hear or watch, we work toward ourselves, but what Bloom calls the "verbal agon for freedom" is not inevitably against that other text, but sometimes toward it as well, as we try to catch it, miss, and come again. The text we make is always tied to, rooted in, that other text, gets its occasion from that other text. Texts exist: they unfold or keep secrets. They go on unfolding and enfolding while we're not watching. They slip away.

Sometimes when I watch and try to get the look and name of people, places, things, events, I only discover what the world already knows, and take a long time learning that. A long time ago I learned from rhetoricians what I took to be a useful little strategy, called the *oratio*, for writers and speakers as they planned what they would say. Originally formulated from the practice of public speakers, the *oratio* proposed certain steps for students and practitioners to take in their discourses. One begins with an *exordium*, concentrating on getting an audience's attention, revealing one's own good intentions, securing some willingness to listen (whence, I suppose, so many jokes at the beginning of speeches and sermons). Then one provides *narratio*, an account of the background and occasion for the discourse. Next comes the *propositio*, the thesis to be presented or point to be argued, which may be followed by the *partitio*, a forecast of the steps to be taken in the ensuing discussion (I expect we've all heard politicians promise that there are "three points that have to be considered"). Then one presents the *confirmatio*, proofs and evidence for the proposition, and the *refutatio*, refutation of opposing views. There's room then for *digressio*, the introduction of illustrative or supporting material from outside the realm of the discussion. *Peroratio* ends the discourses with summary, reiteration of key points, and a call for action. It's a nice scheme, made pleasanter by the movability of the parts as occasion and emphasis require. It is enacted again and again in Western discourse. Richard Lanham remarks in *A Handlist of Rhetorical Terms* that the structure "has influenced the way we think and argue, of course, in every instance where we argue a case," and adds that "the form itself is used, albeit unknowingly, by an enormous number of people" and "often can be detected, writ large, where the argumentative element is secondary."

But I was a long time learning that the *oratio* is not just a way of outlining. When I looked again, I learned that the form tells us something about ourselves, more than I had thought. Looking, I thought I began to see that *narratio* is not just a part of a speech;

it is also the form's testimony to what always happens when we speak and to our attempt to lift the inevitable up to the conscious. We're always situated somewhere when we speak, whether or not we have placed ourselves deliberately. Every utterance comes from somewhere, exists in a setting. Every utterance carries a history. *Narratio* calls us into our history, calls our history into our text, tells us to tilt our ears toward the history carried in the other's speech. I slowly begin to learn that *narratio* is not just part of a strategy but is also, more significantly, our recognition, acknowledgment, insistence that we create a world when we speak, staking out claims, making a history. We are not representing reality but making it, and *exordium* and *peroratio* want us to know that we are makers, deliberately commencing a reality and closing our account of it, not at *the* beginning and *the* ending, which can't be found, but at made sites of convenience, where speaker and hearer can convene.

I begin to learn a little about *refutatio*, too. We are not required to be disputatious, but the text of centuries teaches us that we do sometimes make our meaning against others, and sometimes beside and toward and for others, and always in the midst of others.

The *oratio* turns out to be a remarkable exemplification of ourselves. It is our drama and our sermon; it is the human dance. I didn't see that the first time I looked, or the second, or the third, or many times after that.

Someday, I might even see the world I already know, and know it again. If I look for people and places and things and events and learn their names, perhaps I can call them back. Absent their names, it's hard to call things back into any present, as Jenny Joseph shows in "Language Teaching: Naming":

> I walked along an unfamiliar road
> And all around, the birds twittered and danced
> Through hedgerows blowing in a flat-land wind.
> I wished I knew their names and then instead
> Of saying "small, brown, with a spearing beak,
> Taking a little run then going back,

Twittering a note that rose to a whistle then sank,
You know, those birds you see in hedgerows
Somewhere along the road from Hertfordshire"
I could say "thirp" or whatever bird it was,
And you would know in an instant what they were,
How looked, what doing. I'd have caught the birds
In that one word, its name, and all the knowledge
You might have had that I'm not master of
Would straight away be there to help me out,
Naming is power, but now
The birds twitter and dance, change and so escape me.

I might know them and call them back, and more; in their reality I might find a suggestion of my own. If that midden of people, places, things, events keeps opening up to the looker, might I someday be found evident?

Is it only *after*, I wonder, *after* great change that the need to know the name and look of things becomes urgent? Change sometimes seems to assault identity. Perhaps rapid change continuously teases us all into doubt. We have seen momentous changes in the twentieth century. After another great *volkswanderung* we find ourselves at least politically and electronically urban, if still quaintly pastoral in our minds; after great progress we find ourselves still capable of profound foolishness and sometime evil. Perhaps these changes pitched us into a perpetual nostalgia so that we hunt for traces of ourselves in genealogical searches; in coffee-table books that might show us pictures of ourselves, our gear, our places; in antique malls and fleamarkets that might show us the artifacts of our identity. Out at the feathery fringes past the edge, have I participated in the publicly momentous *after* great change? Have changes in my own life touched me so that I thought they were momentarily momentous? Some didn't notice when Icarus fell.

When you keep falling into history, you keep trying to see and to hold on and to learn whether or not you're there. The great calamities, cultural shifts, and redirections of human life — Is it so? Yes, it is so — occur not just once but many times, the macrocosmic reenacting itself, or the other way around, in the microcosmic. The Holocaust happens again and again, in small ways, in large ways, in intense, sometimes agonized, personal ways. Diaspora and *volkswanderung* reoccur in our personal lives. Our culture fell into history in the Renaissance; individual souls must fall into history in their own ways. Petrarch looked as if for the first time upon the ruins of Rome, and when he did so, Western humans, for the first time, discovered through his nostalgic gaze the irrevocable pastness of the past, the alienness and otherness of antiquity. The educational program of the Renaissance humanist is, we know, premised on the notion of "rebirth," the renewal of ancient culture through the recovery of its literature and language. Yet the more the humanist studied the words and world of those before him, the more poignantly he confronted his own failure to understand, to bridge the cultural, linguistic, spiritual distance between himself and his past. "Wherever I turn," Erasmus writes in relation to the ancients, "I see everything changed; I stand on a different stage; I see a different theatre, yes, a different world." Rome lies in ruin; its language closes itself to living speech; its heroes become ghosts. Jay Parini writes that

> Each word we say
> becomes an elegy to what's lost,
> as this raw tree stump recollects the shade
> we still remember from a Sunday picnic
> when the world was green and parents played
> and sorrow was the last thing left to learn.

We cannot speak in the Ciceronian way unless we live in Cicero's world, and we can't. Humanist philosophy struggles to recover the past but turns ultimately to a new methodology for its authority and truth—empiricism and the New Science. Luther and Descartes and Bacon and others made a world on the ruins of the old, loosing themselves from the past, losing themselves to the past. Individual souls must indeed fall into history in their own ways.

And when we fall into history, we lose, or think we lose, ourselves and our sacraments. Historicity seems to invalidate our identity, our authority, our ways of sorting things out. Topology too falters, and we cannot find the places of significance any more: we can't find our landscapes, with or without geographers. Petrarch's Rome, with its splendid Latin eloquence, is ruined. New languages must be found for new cultural settings. Sometimes some of us recognize that a new world exists, born maybe in 1798 or 1914 or 1945 or in whatever year each of us fell into history. Some of us welcome a new world into understanding and celebrate its arrival, even as we know that it, too, will pass. Sometimes we demonstrate the strength to make ourselves in a changing and uncertain world. Sometimes we don't, and spend ourselves searching for old time and our old places and who we were and the authority that was. We do not live in the Eden of an eternal present: things die, and things change.

Is it only *after*, after times of great change, whether great cultural change or our own small, private enactments of great change, that we begin to look so hard for the names and places and things and people we thought we knew? Perhaps disorder rises not from some single trauma — say, distortion of the primal scene, or maybe Oedipus or whoever dating or whatever his mother or whomever — but from change itself.

Change itself, while it may bring joy, generates disorder, grief, nostalgia. We must be at war: change is inevitable and necessary to life, but it also entails a continuous destruction and loss of worlds, great and small, a combat of old habit with new need. Identity is always about to vanish as old worlds go and new worlds come. In the cacophony of conflicting rhetorics, change never ceases. Even in periods of apparent stability, change continues. Often in modern Western culture, urbanized in expectation if not in fact and trying to stabilize its urbanness, rural and pastoral values keep trying to hold their stability, and both the urban and the rural are undercut and destabilized. In the late twentieth century in the United States, some erected statues to John Wayne and elected his impersonator to the presidency. We're never free of change, and we never get entirely used to it. The world is indeterminate; knowledge is not fixed and stabilized; there is no normality. The world is always coming unfixed, and we keep trying to fix it. All of our questions and all of our answers keep hideous and lovely secrets from us because we can mostly speak only in the language of the day, which is still partly yesterday's language, though it can't be, and must be tomorrow's language, though it won't be. Sometimes, after great change, we walk in lonesome valleys, looking for some familiar landmark.

4

Cast of Characters

Sometimes, of course, change seems trivial, entirely personal, and scarcely noticeable. People may seem or be, Stephen Sandy says,

> placid, day by day
> Unmoving as a pond in autumn hills
> Until one morning they see how something's passed
> Through them; commotion hatching at the edges.

Scarcely noticeable, at least until, say, some stark morning or some cold night you discover, say, that you are not who you thought you were, not who you intended to be. Perhaps such changes, nearly always scarcely noticeable, really are trivial and only personal.

Perhaps not.

Perhaps all small changes cause, ensue from, or reenact great changes. A culture has to discover that history happens and we are in it. So do we, before or after, in quiet or crashing ways.

I had thought I'd be Digby, the middle one, faithful and ready. We had no John, no youngest brother, in our family. My brother was Michael, the oldest, the best, Beau Geste. I thought family should stay together, close, intent on love and fidelity, as they were. I forgot to keep the covenant. I'm the one. Later, with a somewhat larger cast of characters, I forgot again, or failed. I'm the one. But the three of them, Michael, Digby, and John, told the way being and brothering and gallantry were supposed to be, while I waited to be good Digby, old Dig.

You remember the story of Percival Christopher Wren's *Beau Geste*. I had it first from my father's recommendation and the book, but Gary Cooper died for its sake; and later, in various remakes, some younger fellows did, too. You remember the story: how, to save the family, Lady Barbara sold the rare Blue Water without telling anyone and kept a false gemstone in its place; how, to save Lady Barbara's reputation, Michael, rare Beau, stole the false gem and, thought a criminal, fled to France to join the Foreign Legion; how good Digby, steady Dig, to save rare Beau's reputation, said he stole the gem, fled to France to claim the guilt; how young John, steady John, to save the names of rare Beau and steady Dig, said he stole the gem, fled to France, and found them; how they went to Africa with the legion; how they practiced war; how two died; how one came back to tell the story.

They told what brothering was, I thought: selfless, forthright, always close. They defined gallantry. Beau watched over young John and died. Young John laid him out there at Fort Zinderneuf. Digby put a dog at his feet and set the flames for a Viking's funeral and then went forthright to die for young John.

I thought it was the way. My brother was Michael, the best, Beau Geste. I had no flair, no wit, but I was willing and would be Digby. We had no John to tell the story. It was the way I thought being and brothering should be, and were, while I waited to be good Digby, old Dig.

Later, I was startled to find that most of humankind had not received the vision. They had defined brothering, I thought, and gallantry, and I was surprised into regret when I learned that the book was as slight as I, and very nearly as new. It was published in 1926, some three years before my parents published me.

Still, it was the way I thought being and brothering and gallantry were, while I waited to be good Digby, old Dig.

But then we had no John to tell the story, my brother didn't know that he was Beau, and after a while I forgot to be Digby.

5

After

After you discover on some stark morning, or maybe on some
cold night, that you have denied what you thought was being, forgotten brothering, and missed gallantry altogether, how do you
escape regret? And nostalgia? "I'm telling you," Denis Johnson
writes,

> it's cold inside the body that is not the body,
> lonesome behind the face
> that is certainly not the face
> of the person one meant to become.

6

Which Text Do We Use in This Course?

I used to see my doctor regularly for physical examinations. I called them yearly checkups, but they were more nearly nineteen-month checkups, or twenty-three-month checkups. The doctor usually seemed content and unsurprised with what he found. I, on the other hand, was always startled, for what he found when he peered and thumped and listened and prodded, when his needle drew blood, and when his machine looked inside, was not what I had taken to his office.

"Blood pressure's nice and normal," he'd say, "a notch or two on the low side."

"Pulse is strong and steady," he'd report, "and I notice you can slow it still more by breathing deeply and relaxing. Your cardiogram is good."

"Cholesterol, sugar, and uric acid are all right in the middle of normal," he'd say, and smile, pleased with me as evidence that he's a good doctor.

He'd be pleased, but I'd be startled, for he missed a lot. He hadn't found the two mortal illnesses that I suffer from each year. I would withhold any description of my symptoms so that I could test the accuracy of his diagnosis. Neither had his examination caught, apparently, the vigorous intensity of my insides.

Perhaps it was the rest I'd usually had before I saw him. Perhaps that eased me enough for him to miss the mark in diagnosis.

I always, of course, made an appointment long ahead of time. Customarily, I arrived early for my appointment. Customarily, he was running late, with five patients ahead of me, plus emergencies, plus consulting calls. Since he is successful, the chairs in his waiting room are uncommonly comfortable. Customarily, I was able to take a nice nap, indeed sometimes had to be shaken into consciousness when it was finally my turn.

Perhaps it was a mistake to go alone. "Some things," Wayne Dodd says, "are dangerous"

> to do alone:
> go swimming, run a chainsaw,
> be married,
> fish a fast mountain stream, miles from any road.

I should have taken someone with me, if I could have found a witness, someone to give testimony to who I am, if I could have found a witness. The doctor didn't find me. Inside here, where I am, you see, I am full of disciplined zeal. I am intense, strong, abrupt, impatient, angry, contrary, determined, earnest, maybe even visionary, and, oh yes, intense, especially intense. That's who I am, but he didn't find me. He found a slow-pulsed plodder, altogether normal, easygoing.

I took one patient to the doctor, and he found another. I didn't have a witness. My well-being evidenced his efficiency, and he was pleased. "There, there," he said, "it's all right. I'm sure you're intense down in there somewhere." He didn't find me. I'm alone again, without a witness except for people I've never met except on pages. "The remedy for loneliness," Denis Johnson writes,

> is in learning to admit
> solitude as one admits
> the bayonet: gracefully,
> now that already
> it pierces the heart.

The doctor didn't find me. I have no witness. Next week is holiday, Wayne Dodd writes,

> and almost everyone I
> love is somewhere else
> on the earth.

I'm trying to remember that I am who I am, not what he says, and I'm praying what Robert Pack taught:

Which Text Do We Use in This Course? 29

O Lord, keep things the same;
let me be me again in paradise,
reading in my old chair.

The doctor knows who I am. I know who I am. He believes he
has read me. I believe he has missed me, but I'm no longer sure
which text to read. After change, it's hard to tell. Sometimes the
texts are lost.

After the divorce: what she knows is not what I know; what I
was is not what I am; what I am is not what I was; what I was is
not what I was; what I am is not what I am; what I am is not here,
floats somewhere—maybe here, maybe there. I have no witness
and can't testify to my own existence. Won't. Don't know how.
Might. Better not.

Can't.

7

If I Don't Know What Time It Is,
Do I Know Who I Am?

Some of us are preoccupied with the clock and must be *in time, on time, in good time, making good time.* Others seem not to notice much, but all of us are timed, if not all by the clock. Perhaps we become real when we fall into time and know it. If you fall into time, into history, everything is always being lost in the past; all the more quickly, I think, after change, when time always imposes itself faster. Being outside time is not the same as being eternal, transcendent; it may, rather more likely, mean being lost and un-situated. (I am, however, familiar with a certain pleasure found sitting in bars outside time. Good citizens all know why folks sit in bars and drink. We're addicts, they say, or ill or morally rep-rehensible, or we're poor, sad souls looking for company. I go to get lonely, to sit where I'm not known; where thought, even if it's sad, is briefly unoppressed by time; where I can listen to the voices in my head; where I'm briefly not guilty or inadequate. Good citizens don't allow themselves this pleasure.) If you're un-able to keep time straight, that may take you, however briefly, out of time, leave you lost and unlocated.

I have trouble keeping time straight. Sometimes I explain that by saying I'm busy, my mind is too engaged. Sometimes I explain it by saying I'm beyond all that.

Was it what happened in Galveston that disordered time?

The window of my room there gave upon the east, and I couldn't catch the stars I like or see the earth roll away until the last sad light was gone. I couldn't see God, who lives behind my look, beyond the Brazos in the west, sweeps down in northers, chills my back and mind, comes down through maps I do not know.

Sometimes, then, I would wake and stand by the window and

signal the sun to rise and wave the waiting ships into port. Noises would skitter down the hall as the world roused from sleep.

Nobody there knew me.

The ship channel was yonder, the beach there, the Gulf beyond. Beach. Gulf. Galveston. I was in Galveston and a ghost. They didn't know me.

I nevertheless adjusted the world, straightened my bed to make it GI tight, and aligned the papers on my table. I settled the yoke over my shoulders, where the nations dangled. I straightened the harness around my waist where the cities and states and countries and villages and farmhouses and windmills hung. I pulled for slack on the ropes tied to my bones, muscles, gut, where the people twist and turn.

Often by mid-afternoon I had taken two reasonably adequate steps: I started the world in the morning, and later, on the beach, I turned back the water one more time.

I knew that I could not handle these chores indefinitely. Back when the preacher said that I must be my own priest, I took him at his word. I priested well enough, I thought, so I took steps to see this priest was heard in prayer: I decided I'd also be God. Then I found that the prayers this priest might say did not suffice, for he had gone to Hell, and had no God to pray to anyway.

Or was it the other?

As I am given to understand the matter, electric shock treatments are a version of oxymoron. Two worlds are brought into collision, and the force creates new meaning not in either taken separately. In some forms of therapy, the briefest possible electric shock is administered to the patient through electrodes applied to the skull. This may be done bilaterally, with an electrode placed on each side of the skull, or unilaterally, with both electrodes placed on the same side so that the shock is felt in the nondominant side of the brain. The bilateral mode works faster but is also more likely to produce momentary confusion and some memory lapses. The unilateral mode is slower, but it produces less confusion and fewer memory lapses. Both short-term and long-term memory failures may, however, accompany either mode. When the shock is administered, it has to be sufficient to cause a convulsive reaction, however mild, or there is no discernible effect on the patient. Electric shock is chiefly used for its presumed value in lifting depression. The convulsion is expected to uncover or to animate dormant or dulled or ineffectual thought paths, lifting depression by jamming other thought paths against the depressed path the brain has been taking. This sudden encounter of diversities is presumed to create a new set of possibilities for the mind, as oxymoron does. And all of this can begin to happen in far less time than we might think—from the time the patient stretches out on the appointed bed, through the injection that reduces the violence of the convulsion and induces sleep, through the shock, and on to awakening, often in less than five minutes.

Was it what happened in Galveston that brought disorder and confused my time? Probably not. Probably I was already disordered. Perhaps I have trouble keeping time straight because I have trouble keeping time straight.

After change, great or small, the confusion of time is momentous to me, and I am lost, unsituated. I try to get the right clock, to enter time, to be in time, but I also yearn to mark the days, to keep time by looking carefully and deliberately at minutes, hours, days, by celebrating them. Perhaps if I had kept the time better, had marked the days better, I'd know when *after* is and keep time straight.

That time.

That time in August 1977: They left.

Early in the month David was married, and he was gone. Late in the month we loaded Mindy's needments and took her, she and I and Cathy, to SMU for her freshman year, and she was gone. At the end of the month we loaded Cathy's needments in the rented van, and she drove Cathy to Evanston to begin graduate school, and Cathy was gone.

Have I got the time straight?

That time in September 1977? Cathy called from Evanston, wanting to know if she could come home for a weekend. School didn't start at Northwestern until late September. The quarter system disorders the semester system.

Have I got the time straight?

Was it October 1977 when we rode the train to Chicago? I had to see publishers. We met Cathy at the Hilton in Evanston. From the window we watched her come down the street from class.

Have I got the time straight?

Was it Thanksgiving 1977? Cathy came home for the holiday, and we were all together for a moment that Thursday. She flew back into a blizzard and ice storm, the beginning of Chicago's record year for snow.

I don't have the time straight. Cathy came home. Was it summer 1978? Good years followed. All close by. We went to the library on Saturdays. I didn't keep the time straight. Was I being important?

Was it January 1981 when she went to Washington? I believe so. I was still being the dean. She went with sparse holdings, found a job, a place to live. At spring break we filled a rented van with the rest of her belongings and took them to her.

Then was it that summer of 1981 that I went to Sadler Hall to be important?

August 19, 1981.

Mindy was married in February 1982. Cathy came back for the wedding. I believe I have it right. Then was it summer 1982 when we drove to Washington up along the Blue Ridge Parkway, in the Chevrolet, and home by a different route, down through West Virginia and out? I believe so.

I was in the hospital in Galveston all through the spring of 1983? I believe I have it right.

Cathy came back while I was gone? Time is not disordered; memory is disrupted.

In the hospital again in the spring of 1984?

May 19, 1985.

May 19, 1987.

On Saturday, October 10, 1987, I took Roberta to the airport, then went to the library downtown, then to the office to work, then to Pulido's for dinner, then to Abernathy's to drink. In the afternoon it was hot. In the little while I was at Abernathy's, the first noticeable norther of the year came in. When I came out, the wind was up and it was cool, and leaves and dust were whirling.

On Sunday morning, October 11, 1987, at about 8:40, Patsy called from the airport to tell me Cathy was gone, would reach Washington around 2:00 P.M.

Don't leave me in the dark, Cathy. But I left you.

That Sunday evening it was uncommonly quiet everywhere — on the campus, where I had worked most of the day, at Abernathy's, where I went to drink. For a while I was the only customer. Few things stirred.

Cathy is gone. My family is gone. I am gone.

By Monday evening, October 12, 1987 — have I got the time straight? — I'm in reasonably bad shape and isolated from the world. All is quiet. The world is elsewhere and I'm in jeopardy, and I think how much nicer it is to be drunk than it would be to be an alcoholic.

Have I got the time straight?

8

Dislocation

Tiny tectonic shifts occur after (and with and before) change,
and continents or chairs disappear.

In times past, I have sometimes known where to sit at funerals,
known the aisle to take, and pew, or chair, or bench at least, have
known where to put myself for grief, or for the public rendition
of grief.

If you're not family, you find a nice place, maybe in the inconspicuous middle, maybe toward the back, maybe off to an
unobtrusive side, and you sit down and be quiet.

If you're family, someone tells you where to sit, or you just
know, from the practice of generations. At the Jayton Baptist
Church, that time in 1938 when Grandpa died, I think we sat in
the middle at the front. But how could it have been the middle?
That little church was surely not wide enough for three sections
of pews, and if there weren't three sections, there couldn't have
been a middle. Still, it feels like the middle, there where we were,
where my father cocked his head to the side and looked up, the
way folks do when they mean not to cry, where as the service
ended Uncle Bill fell into a fit of crying, where Aunt Mary did
not acknowledge that crying existed. We went back after all those
years for Grandma's funeral—when was it? 1953? 1954? 1956? why
the hell don't I know—and it still seems like the middle, but the
little church surely wasn't wide enough for three sections of pews,
so how could there have been a middle?

At St. Stephen Presbyterian Church, if you're family, you sit at
the front on the left. I haven't been there yet. I don't want to be
there. Perhaps I won't.

If you're family and you go to a funeral home, someone tells
you where to sit and when. Sometimes it's in front in the middle.
Sometimes it's in front off to a side, where you're shielded from
the stares of common mourners.

If you're to bear the pall with five others, someone tells you where to sit, leads you there, arranges how you sit, tells you when to rise, what to do, fixes it so that tall is by tall, short by short, medium by medium, so we'll all look moderately nice, too many times, too many times.

I have sometimes known where to sit at funerals, known the aisle to take, and pew, or chair, or bench at least, have known where to put myself for grief, or for the public rendition of grief.

But where will I sit now at funerals? Where is the place I'm supposed to be? I don't have a place.

Suppose her mother dies. Or mine. Am I not to mention the possibility? The possibility is there, with me, with her, with them. Suppose her mother dies. Or mine. Then where do I sit? Where is the place I'm supposed to be?

Suppose it's her mother, who fed me, cared for me, even if she didn't always listen to me. Do I go and join as if family? Seems unlikely. I'd not be wanted. Do I find a nice place, maybe in the inconspicuous middle, maybe toward the back, maybe to an un-obtrusive side, and sit down, and be quiet?

Suppose it's my mother, who fed me, cared for me in her funny way, even if she didn't always listen to me. Do I go and take my rightful place as family in the middle in front, in the front on the side, in some discreet alcove, shielded from the stares of common mourners? Seems improper. She was family to my mother, too, would want to be there, I think. Do I absent myself from what's left of family, leave my place with family for her, what was hers, go and find a nice place, maybe in the inconspicuous middle, maybe toward the back, maybe to an unobtrusive side, sit down, and be quiet?

We have scattered, she and I, she to her exodus, I to mine, and there is no next time in Mannheim, or on Stadium Drive, or in the Croton Breaks.

Then where do I sit at funerals? Where is the place I'm supposed to be? Where is my place?

9

The Farm Is Gone

Wherever my place is, I do appear to be supposing that after great change we need to know the name and look and situation of things more urgently. Change seems to disorder time, to alter the landscape, to assault identity. Perhaps rapid change always brings us to doubt. Perhaps the momentous changes of the twentieth century pitched us into a perpetual nostalgia so that we hunt for traces of ourselves, our times, our landscapes. Out at the feathery fringes past the edge, have I participated in the publicly momentous *after* great change? Have changes in my own life touched me so that I think they are at least momentarily momentous? Did Icarus fall without witness? Was I a plowman who never looked up to see?

I have come at times to suppose that the great calamities, cultural shifts, and redirections of human life occur again and again, the large reenacting itself in the small, or the other way around. If I look at public change, will I understand myself better? If I look at private change, will I understand the world better? If I have been part of great change, or an echo of great change, can I be released a little from culpability from my own crimes of commission and omission?

When I try to get over yonder to see how things look back here, I sometimes am mostly simple and mostly provincial; sometimes I think that I've not been on the edge of change, that I've not participated even in small ways in great change. I don't in fact know whether it's arrogance or shame that causes me to suppose that the little can reflect, echo, or embody the large—arrogance to suppose that the particular is important to the general, shame to want to hide my particulars inside the culture. I have no athlete's laurels. I have not been to war, though near. I have not watched when mother, father, sister, died as bombs fell or gas hissed. I cannot match either the expectation or the loss of great migrations. All those thousands upon thousands who left Russia for the United States in the last decades of the nineteenth century: what did they look toward? Whom did they leave? In his book *Goodbye to a River*, John Graves tells of finding old letters spilled from a broken trunk in an abandoned cabin above the Brazos River. One is dated April 17, 1899. In it, Elnora sends news from Hood's Cove, Kentucky, to Addie in Texas, then goes on: "I do not know where Time *goes* and when he said the other Day that it was *Twenny Five Years* since You All want out to Texas and I began to cry Dear Sister, because I do not *believe* that we are Like to see Each Other any more."

Still, the changes and losses that I have known, though I haven't known them well enough, seem real to me, sometimes seem grinding to me, and may at least be a little like the changes that have occurred out yonder in the world. I have been in great migration, the great shift from the rural and reputedly pastoral to the urban that has been going on in this country for a hundred years and may now be over—if we are not all geographically and politically urban, we have been mostly urbanized socially by television—though I think we have not yet come to understand all it has meant to us. More than a few have argued that the apparent success of Ronald Reagan in two elections was owed in large part to his apparent articulation of the values of a rural, pastoral, Rockwellian America (one that existed mostly in the movies) against what some saw as the wild changes of the 1960s and 1970s. The movement that some have called conservative, others have called reactionary, and others have called fundamentalist is not over yet, whatever its name turns out to be, for we are still, while mostly living in one mostly urbanized world, mostly thinking and feeling in that other world that seems mostly pastoral.

In 1939 I moved with my father and mother and older brother from West Texas, from a little town of fewer than 700 souls and less water, to a city of more than 200,000 people, and I've been a little lost ever since. During these later years I've gone back to learn the name and look and situation of things, but the things I've looked for aren't there, and when I look at my maps, I'm not there either. Once I was there, and once my people were scattered over parts of three counties. The last are gone. My grandfather died. About a year later his farmhouse burned. Then my definite aunt and my gentle uncle moved away to the city. They were the last. Now they are gone. The wind passes over the places where they were, and they are gone, and the places where they were will know them no more. I remember fondly what probably never was.

Still, although what I take to be radical changes have astonished me, most would say my life has been simple and sheltered. The changes have been real enough to me, and the losses, so real that I have to keep checking to see traces, remains, vestiges, evidences of myself. My desk dictionary defines *compulsion* as "an irresistible impulse to perform an irrational act." Is what one does compulsive, do you reckon, if one can still talk about it? I don't know. I do know that I can't stop reading myself like braille to learn if I'm still there. I try to be unobtrusive; I don't know how many, if any, have noticed, but I read my own braille time after time—left hip pocket first to be sure my tobacco pouch is there; then right hip pocket to check my handkerchief; then left front pocket to know my wallet's there (and when I'm alone I also have to look inside the wallet); then right front pocket to be sure of my keys, knife, three rocks, and a silver dollar; and last, my shirt pocket to touch two fountain pens, a pencil, a ballpoint pen, my little spiral notebook, and my money. Not all of my money—just what I've put out for running expenses. If your resources are, as they say, limited and might end soon if luck and work don't hold out, and one's no chancier than the other, despite what they say, then you must marshal your resources, as they say, to make them last; and it's hard to marshal, mind the horses, hard to count, to keep your cash, when you're not quite sure that you are there, not quite sure that you can count. Early in the day I put money in my shirt pocket behind the little spiral notebook; enough, I hope, to last until sleep. I mustn't get my wallet out unless I'm alone and watching: I might lose it all, lose track, lose cash, identify, all, must keep myself confined to my shirt pocket while I come and go, while I touch my pockets to tell I'm there. If I don't come and go, I might be here.

And so might they all, come for a minute, go, be gone.

Oh my daughter, I check the weather reports every morning in the newspaper, but I can't be sure I have the weather right where you are, for I'm not there. If I were there, I might mistake the air or miss the rain, might forget the cold or slant of snow. I might think that what I see is weather. I check the local paper, see what happened yesterday, what might come today, and I wonder: Are you warm? And are you dry? Must you go far in the cold? But I don't know if I've got my worrying timed to your weather. Perhaps the front I read about today is already gone, or stalls to chill you sometime late tonight. The weather page, you know, tells the high, the low, and the state of the sky for diverse geographies—Fort Worth and Dallas, North Texas, West Texas, South Texas, but not East Texas—reports on Texas cities, U.S. cities, tells yesterday, today, and tomorrow (one with some certainty). Tomorrow's report will be somewhat more accurate about today's. It tells about U.S. cities, about your city, and then about those far and foreign cities with strange isobars and wind prevailing otherwise. I trust the newspaper's report. It's what I have to trust. Can you send word? Have I got my worry timed to your map? And still not remembered that I can't keep you safe?

They're gone.

I've been in migration, and watched migration pass me. I've been sheltered, not in or on the edge of great public change, and still have heard the footsteps, seen the fading dust cloud of diaspora, felt at least a candle's worth of holocaust, heard echoes, sensed reverberations, always sheltered and at a distance. No, not always. Perhaps I *am* the twentieth century, mostly shallow, mostly superficial, incapable of great art or much of anything, genuinely, thoroughly mediocre, watching at a distance as the trivial becomes monstrous, the monstrous trivial. Perhaps I am the twentieth century, and Freud was my father. He was here sometime, though probably not in the right season to sire me. Still, you never know: he was crafty and sometimes wise, and might have done the job. On Mondays I doubt it. He and my mother wouldn't have moved in the same circles. She probably wouldn't have consented. Besides, he smoked cigars and was old enough to have been her father, too. I got the genes remembered almost right. I inherited the maladies he created as best I could, though I failed in some particulars. But maybe the little girl from Texas wasn't my mother. Maybe I wasn't born. Probably I had to be invented so the whole entire total twentieth century could enact its foolishness, find a place for its trivialities, changes, losses, sins. If that is so, that makes necessity my mother, my home the dry land where I began.

A hospital ought not to be for just a few. If we had a party for all who were here before, for those here now, and for those who need to come, we'd have such crowds as never were before. I don't know how we'd feed and bed the world, or salve the hurts the crushing crowd would cause. All are patients. No bread or fish is waiting. On a day that will come, the dead will pile around us, and the trees will die, and the grass we mowed so neatly will go yellow and dry, and the tumbleweeds will shift and bounce before a dry wind, and the desert will win, and all of us will die.

I wonder if I have ever seen any of the truth. I wonder if I have ever seen my own doubt accurately. Are we always in doubt after great change? Is every moment of our existence a moment that follows great change? Sometimes I have to judge that what I see is always and only what *I* see, that I can never catch a truth from out there, that I can never catch what's outside myself or count for anything outside myself. Yet I sometimes know that the world's harmonies and cacophonies sound in me, and I sometimes suppose that the world rings to my tune. I don't know whether I puzzle in arrogance or shame. Can I ever know? Know anything for sure? I'm certain at moments that it was just my binge, my change, my loss, but then for moments I think that the world reeled and taught me. Has it always and only been *my* time disorder, *my* little tectonic shifts, *my* puzzlement about identity? Yes, of course, and no. Can I ever know? Know anything for sure? Will I begin to know if I look closely enough, accurately enough within and without? Can I get situated to see? If I see, will I acknowledge? I'm pretty sure that the grandmother is right in Fred Chappell's poem "My Grandmother Washes Her Feet."

"O what's the use," she said, "Water seeks
Its level. If your daddy thinks that teaching school
In a white shirt makes him a likelier man,
What's to blame? Leastways, he won't smother
Of mule-farts or have to starve for a pinch of rainfall.
Nothing new gets started without the old's
Plowed under, or halfway under."

Will I know when—if—I know that there is an *in here* and a *yon-der*, when—if—I know that there is an *after*, a *later*, a *yonder*? Yes, of course, and no. I think identity wavers out there elsewhere, and time breaks, and landscapes shift and erode. Perhaps we all wander, lost in migration, trying to find ways to transform ourselves, trying to fix ourselves, to repair the world.

10

The Personnel Office

Reports vary. That's what reports always do, but after a while you begin to catch a common story from them: about 75 percent of college graduates in this country wind up in careers unconnected with their undergraduate major field of study, and Americans average about three major job changes or career shifts during their working years. I've stayed in one place for thirty years, but job changes, at least it seems to me, have been abrupt and startling. If you're sentenced to hang and then reprieved, if you catch leprosy and then are cured, it tends first to concentrate your attention, then to addle your brain. Things move around. You learn surprising things about yourself and others. I want to believe I am not alone in my response. I think I'm not.

I came to where I am, wherever that may be, thirty years ago to be an English teacher, and eventually became a professor, though I had, I thought, already been professing. Perturbations and aberrations occurred along the way, some brief, some not. I was chairman of the English Department for ten years, dean of the College of Arts and Sciences for five years, and Associate Vice President for Whatever Came Up for two years. I pursued this course because they told me if I stayed around and kept at it, sooner or later I would get steady work. About three years ago I resigned all that and fell partway back to grace and all the way back to the English Department. These shifts brought surprising discoveries.

Example. One day while I was still working in what they're pleased here to call the "central administration," I ran into a young woman named Carol Courtney, and the encounter brought into question my conception of the cosmos.

I didn't really run into her, of course. We didn't collide and career off the walls. Rather, we chanced to meet just outside the door of Sadler Hall 208, she just coming out, I about to enter.

That in itself was not surprising—we both worked then in Sadler Hall 208. What raised doubts about my conception of the cosmos was something she said.

Before that, I had the landscape of the universe pretty well worked out. I had long before noticed that I customarily referred to places in the north as *up*: I'd go *up* to Chicago or New York or Washington or Denton. Places to the south always seemed to be *down*: I'd go *down* to Houston or Austin or Cleburne. If I referred to places in the east, they were *over*: one goes *over* to Vicksburg or Atlanta or Dallas. And it seemed to me that if one goes to the west, it's always *out*: I go *out* to Santa Fe or Los Angeles or Muleshoe. That seemed to settle things. If north is *up* and south is *down* and east is *over* and west is *out*, then it's pretty clear where the center of things is: I'm it. The Great Divide runs up my chest, and everything is located from wherever I happen to be standing. If I were in Houston, Fort Worth would be *up*. If I were in Chicago, Fort Worth would be *down*. If I were in Dallas, Fort Worth would be *out*. It all seemed settled.

But my encounter with Carol Courtney brought my geography into question. She had just come out of Sadler Hall 208. By way of keeping me posted, she said, "Hi there, I'm going up the hall to Political Science." I asked her why she'd said "*up* the hall to Political Science." She looked at me strangely and said, "I don't know; I guess I never stopped to think about it." So I asked her, "If you were already up in Political Science, how would you talk about returning here?" She looked at me strangely again and said, "Well, I guess I'd say, 'I've got to get back down the hall to work.' Why do you ask?"

I didn't much want to give her an honest or complete answer, and so I invented a sensible answer, "No particular reason—I'm just interested in linguistic patterns."

She seemed willing to let it go with that, but she had raised a serious question in my mind. What she actually said was not a problem. Sadler Hall 208 is at the south end of the second floor of the building. The Political Science Department is at the north end of the second-floor hall. According to my cosmology, if one leaves Sadler Hall 208 headed for the Political Science Department, it is fitting to say, "Hi there, I'm going *up* the hall to Political Science," because that's going north. If one leaves Political Science headed for 208, it is fitting to say, "I've got to get back *down* the hall," because that's going south. So far, so good.

But I couldn't get the matter out of my mind. I went on into my office, which was inside the nest of offices numbered Sadler Hall 208, sat down, and pondered prepositions. The human brain is a marvelous organ and a wonderful comfort: if a fellow has it in mind not to work, he can usually count on his brain to devise a way of avoiding work and a justification for doing so. I sat there for a while wondering if I really did have things straight. Ms. Courtney's *up* and *down* seemed to authenticate my geographical scheme, but I made a list of places on the campus and asked myself whether or not my up-north/down-south/over-east/out-west system held true for all.

It didn't.

The geography I started with simply doesn't work part of the time. Sometimes there's a good reason, a legitimate accounting for its inadequacy. But sometimes there's not—sometimes the geography just shifts. Geologists who study plate tectonics apparently understand how continents and pieces of continents move around, or seem to. I don't. Sometimes the landscape just shifts.

Sometimes there's a good reason. If I started out the door of Sadler Hall 208 and announced "I'm going down the hall," *down* in that instance didn't signify south. It meant I was going *up* the hall, or north. Direction wasn't the issue in this instance. "Going down the hall" is a euphemism for going to the restroom, which is something that happened in those days even to those of us who otherwise walked on water (collected in small puddles). In those days I would have said, were I going to any of those places, that I was going *down* to the Health Center, *down* to the stadium, or *down* to the coliseum, even though all of those places are west and should be *out*. However, each of those places is literally down the hill from Sadler Hall. I would also have said that I was going *down* to Rogers Hall or *down* to the Bass Building, even though they are east and ought to be *over*, because they are down the hill the other way. Those places don't fit the geography I started with, but for good enough reasons, I thought then.

Some places on campus did hold true to my old scheme. I'd go *down* to the Bailey Building, and it's south. I'd go *over* to the Winton-Scott Science Building, to the Sid Richardson Building, and to Brite Divinity School, and that was appropriate, for all are east from Sadler Hall 208.

But then there were other places that my old geography didn't accommodate. For example, I would go *over* to Ed Landreth Auditorium, to the Moudy Building, to Jarvis Hall, and to Reed Hall, and that's all wrong because all four are north and should have been *up*. I would go *over* to the Speech and Hearing Clinic, and that's all wrong because it's northwest and should have been either *up* or *out*. I would go *over* to the Rickel Center, and that was clearly wrong; it's west and should be *out*. The library doesn't make any sense at all. I didn't go *up*, *down*, *over*, or *out*—I just went *to* the library.

My geography just wasn't working. I remember sitting there, trying to figure out what had gone wrong with my prepositions.

Finally, it occurred to me that, apparent anomalies notwithstanding, perhaps my old geography still held, though there were slippages in the scheme. Even if the prepositions didn't always work right, all the usages seemed to have one thing in common. Every usage suggested the possibility of both a departure and a return. If I went *up*, I could usually come *down*. If I went *over*, I could usually come back *out*. That made everything all right. I was still the center of the universe.

And then, a little later, I figured out that everybody in the world was probably busy using prepositions in his or her own way. I couldn't count on all of them to use my system, not at all. That being so, I began to reckon that there are many universes swirling here, each speaker the center of his or her own. It's little wonder that we sometimes have trouble speaking across the spaces that separate us, though there are times when word gets *down* or *up* or *over* or *out*, or even *through*.

At any rate, though I presently felt safe at the center, there was another problem with prepositions. Some of them probably *don't* signify the possibilities of a departure and a return to the speaker's own center. When I was young, I heard many hymns about how things were *up* in Heaven or *down* in Hell. I don't think the hymnodists were talking about north and south. I heard songs that said "I'm going to cross *over* into Canaan," or "I am just going *over* Jordan." Such usages, contrary to my little geography, seemed to signify departure but not return; and that, in turn, seemed to suppose that there is some center other than the speaker's own breastbone. But that, I thought, was another story and probably had little to do with encountering Ms. Courtney in the hall, and besides, I was not ready or able to talk about the matter then. You might say I was not *up* to it at the moment, or couldn't get *down* to it. You might say I was all *out*, or *over*.

Perhaps confusion came because I had changed offices too many times and my prepositions had fallen in arrears of my location. But more than the landscape changed. I began to discover, once I was back in the English Department, a leftover from administrative work, that I was somebody I hadn't been, that I wasn't somebody I was before, that I had been somebody I wasn't, or whatever. Identity and its appurtenances also shift with change, though after change one is sometimes laden with leftovers. Sometimes one *is* a leftover.

Leftovers, however, can be interesting, even if that class of things includes myself and yesterday's casserole. I don't mean by calling them leftovers to malign those who leave administrative positions to return to full-time faculty positions. In general, I think they ought to be congratulated on their departure from the apparent university and their return to the real university. Still, despite my own currently pleasurable circumstances, I find the subject more than a little melancholy, and so chose the term "leftovers" for its suggestion of shards, artifacts, remnants, and the sorry prospect of tasting the same Christmas turkey too many times.

What happens to leftovers? I can answer inadequately for myself by mentioning some changes that have come, some near traumas that I have or have not avoided, some twists and turns of identity that have startled me a little.

Having enough coffee hasn't been a problem. I had coffee before. I have coffee now.

I've had the strength to answer the telephone for myself and to fetch my own mail, but I miss the reassurance I found when someone came in early each morning to tell me who I was.

I've learned that having one's own travel budget, however small, is nicer than not having one, and provides some testimony that one actually exists.

I'm still puzzled by this and that. Faculty people, for example, are supposed to write and to publish. Administrative people mostly are not. They have decided to be someone else, and some of them are likely to frown at you if they catch you writing while you're an administrator. They wonder, I think, if you know who you are; and they wonder, I think, why you aren't making snappy executive decisions.

Up until five o'clock one Friday afternoon I was apparently a marvelous public speaker. At eight o'clock on the following Monday I apparently was not. While I was an administrator I sometimes seemed to be making a speech wherever three people (counting myself) were gathered. On request, I spoke at banquets, retreats, meetings of honor societies, meetings of prospective students, and very nearly anywhere else, and I rejoiced in the grand compliments I received on those grand occasions. I came to suspect that, by God, those people might be right, and maybe I was a magnificent speaker. But then that Monday morning came, and I wasn't. I waited, but no invitations came. I'll have to admit that I feel no great loss in this regard, but so rapid a shift does tend to leave a fellow mildly confused.

All the more, I'd guess, because I had allowed myself, sometimes shamefully, sometimes shamelessly, to participate in a common form of behavior that would be vile if it weren't so foolish, would be foolish if it weren't so vile. I succumbed to flattery, to self-deception, and to a whole range of transparent behaviors that everyone pretended were not transparent. I wanted to believe that all the invitations to speak and to attend balls and lovely black-tie dinners were for me, for my own wise and charming self, and I often deceived myself, wallowing in the flattery of attention. I knew that those who invited me to do things and to be places did so partly because they were kind and attentive and partly because I was kind of nice myself, was not habitually illiterate, and did not commonly scratch myself in public or spit on the floor. At the same time, I also knew that they invited me chiefly not because I was myself but because I was a dean or whatever. All of us acted as if position had nothing to do with invitations. All of us knew better. All of us, myself first of all, were to some extent or another participating in habits of deference to position, bad enough in themselves, but worse because they all too easily become habits of separation, distrust, and even fear. All of us were sometimes foolish. I was worse: I succumbed to flattery directed not at me but at a position. I deceived myself even while I knew I was deceiving myself, and now I respond to it all in churlish ways, flailing about not because I succeed where others don't but because I fail as they do. What a strange world.

Up until that Friday afternoon I "knew things," including cabalistic designs and high secrets. No one should ever minimize the uncommonly seductive appeal of "knowing things," of "being in on things." This powerfully seductive need to be *in* ultimately seems to feed vanity and to promote self-serving behavior, and I lusted to fill both appetites. The next Monday morning I was not *in*, not privy to the secrets of state. What a falling off that was! However, there was compensation: I no longer had to be *tough*, which I hadn't managed successfully anyway.

I found a great many other faults in myself along the way. Some of them were faults on both Friday and Monday, some on Friday but not on Monday, some on Monday but not on Friday. All are mine. Some "leftovers" may take up their new duties with great relief and happiness. Some will shuffle along well enough. Some, I suppose, *should* be "leftovers" and will grow mold as fast as can reasonably be expected. Were technology more advanced, we might consider freezing some in the hope that a new use for them may be discovered later. I'm not too keen on this possibility, though others may find it promising. I do know that when the landscape changes under your feet, you may not turn out to be who you thought you were.

II

Can I Get a Witness?

My crises are mostly, but not all, piddling, though they are dear and dire enough for me. Questions about whether or not I exist, or how, or what qualities I have, if any, or what landscape I live in, while not especially momentous to most, are uncommonly interesting to me. They are there before I know they're there. They creep around and in me, sometimes burst upon me, sometimes rising out of great public change or out of private shift, sometimes rising out of sources that, in the minds of some, might not seem to matter.

I had not expected it of literary theorists and critics, but they whittle away at me, taking away what I had, or hoped I had, or hoped I might have, until my features blur and after a while I disappear altogether.

An ancient tool holds down a stack of papers on the table in the corner of my office. A rock implement, it is vaguely like the head of a sledgehammer. It is generally cylindrical, about ten inches long, about three inches in diameter at its middle, and comes to a rough, striated point at one end. The other end has a half-circle indentation that cuts through most of the three-inch thickness. The shape suggests two possible uses. The indentation at one end creates a reasonably comfortable handhold, and the striations at the other end further suggest that it might have been a grinding tool. My three children, each in turn, decided on the other possible use: each in turn carried the thing lashed with a leather thong to a stout stick, which fit neatly into the indentation. It made a formidable club.

That was the history of its reality, created and determined by the narrative we told of it.

Then a colleague from the Geology Department saw it, said no, said it's not a tool, just a funny-shaped rock, wedged for eons against a smaller, harder round rock that eventually wore the indentation. The alternative view enables the viewer to see things differently, or demands that he or she see things differently, denies instrumentality, and deconstructs my rock. The alternative words stop my words, and the reality of the rock changes. The geologist's history effaces my history. Since, I've been quarreling with myself, sometimes petulantly, sometimes foolishly. "Damn well is a tool," I say one day, and "probably isn't" the next.

I had wanted to believe in one thing, you see, and had believed until an alternative view brought my belief into question.

I had wanted to believe, you see, that *ethos*, the character of a speaker or writer, is real and dwells in the text left by the speaker; that it was there—just as Aristotle and, until yesterday, all who came after him had said—and that I could find it and perhaps even leave evidence of my own character in stray words thoughtlessly left behind. Others, however, have been looking with different eyes and have consequently seen things differently, as the geologist saw in my implement only a rock. Diverse others—those who have taught us recently about interpretive communities, about the social construction of discourse, about reader-response theory, for example—have told me in diverse ways that ethos is *not in the text* but in the reader or community, in their projection on the text. They have told me, further, that the writer is not autonomous, but is only part of a social community that constructs and interprets discourse, that the notion of the self as a source of meaning is only a romantic concept (which would probably surprise Alexander Pope), that the language by which we view and construct the world comes from society, not from the individual. Ethos— character in the remaindered text—is at the very least problematic. I can't catch character in the text, it seems clear, not on my own previous terms. That may mean that I can't ever be real to you, or you to me, or the other to either of us.

And the consequence is that I am frightened. As Joan Rivers might say, "Can we talk?" If ethos is not in the text, if the author is not autonomous, I'm afraid that I've lost my chance not just for survival hereafter (that happened some time ago) but also for identity now. Poststructuralist thought announces the death of the author: language writes us, rather than the other way around, and interpretation prevails rather than authorship. We have been, whether knowingly or not, whether directly or not, part of a twenty-five-hundred-year-old tradition that allowed and encouraged us to believe that character is in the text, that authors do exist, that they can be in their words and own them even in the act of giving them away. Now literary theorists both compelling and influential tell us that it is not so, that character exists, if at all, only in the perceiving minds of readers; that authors, if they exist, do so somewhere else, not in their words, which have already been interpreted by their new owners. Language is orphaned from its speaker: what we once thought was happening has been disrupted. Authors, first distanced, now fade away into nothing. Not even ghosts, they are projections cast by readers. "They" out there want, that is to say, to take my own voice away from me and give such meaning as there might be over entirely to whoever might show up as an interpreter. "They" want me—and you and all those others—to die into oblivion if we should manage to scribble something, never to be reborn in a voice for some reader, but to vanish before that reader's construction/deconstruction/reconstruction of the small things we leave behind.

Can I get a witness? Can you? Or she, or he? In texts that are absent?

Will anyone notice that I may be here, that this is the way I talk, that this is what in my mind passes for thinking, that this may be myself? Life is real, and the artificial compartments we create for it don't work. What gets said in one place keeps slopping over and meaning something in other places. I'm talking about my own identity now, the nuttiness that is mine.

And yet, and yet: I have written as much to hide as to reveal, have written so that I might show the writing to others and *not* be required to show myself. There's more to me than meets the eye, and less. Whatever is in here might be terrible to see, worse to reveal. A piece of writing can be revelatory, exploratory; more are than we have acknowledged. It can also be a substitute for the unspeakable, a closure, not a revelation.

Not so long ago, a book of personal essays that I wrote was published. They are mostly about West Texas. Four reviewers so far have commented on it—my wife, my brother, and two newspaper reviewers. Three of them were favorably disposed. One of the newspaper reviewers said some moderately nice things about what he was pleased to call my "voice" and "character" in the book. I was tickled and danced a little jig.

And I was startled when I realized what else was in my mind, startled when I realized that I was already talking back to the reviewer. "Listen, you out there," I was saying, "don't think I'm so easy to catch. There's more to me than meets the eye, and less. You'll not catch me so quickly."

At the moment I want and need ethos—character—in the text so that I can be real, I deny that it is there. I am not here, but elsewhere.

Most things aren't ever over. Few things are easily real, easily what we say they are. Fewer things, I hope, come to nothing. Ethos may yet be here. I may yet be here. Perhaps. Yes.

12

Show and Tell

I'm still here, I believe, though under question, and some parts may be missing.

On most university campuses, faculty members are expected to keep—and most generally want to keep—a little record of our work, regularly updated. I keep such a record. It's called a *curriculum vitae*. It's supposed to show my education and experience, publications, and public presentations. Part of my little record is incomplete, and now, I think, I'll never be able to recover what's missing.

And so, when I look, I sometimes don't know what to make of myself.

How could I have left, given the way I think I feel about family and place? How could I have violated what I at least think I believe? How could I have caused doubt and hurt? How could someone love me if I am selfish, perhaps evil, possibly only commonplace, trivial, maybe invisible. Sometimes I don't know what to make of myself, yet there is no self but the self I make.

Do I fail to show enough, to tell enough? Do I show only effect, not cause? If I don't provide enough referents, will you wonder why I act and think as I do? Have I not made plain what I react to, or against? I haven't explained a divorce. I haven't explained about the psychiatric ward in Galveston. I haven't explained why I am lost to my daughter, and she to me. What is hidden among what is revealed? Do you need to know more? I may not tell.

Looked at from outside, events of my life are ordinary enough in the late twentieth century. I was lost in work among conflicting languages, wanting attention; and when you want attention, there is no such thing as enough. I spent some months in a hospital. I was separated from my family and place, momentarily lost to all of my children, entirely estranged from one of them. I was divorced. I remarried. Ordinary enough, in the late twentieth century.

But nothing is ordinary. Come inside my head.

Much is missing there, too. I put down dates so that I can keep them. August 1977. August 19, 1981. Spring 1983. May 19, 1985. May 19, 1987. October 12, 1987. Many are missing. I wish I could keep everything.

Much is missing from my little academic record, my curriculum vita. For a period of about fifteen years I didn't keep a record of public presentations. During that time I read papers at academic conferences, made speeches, gave lectures, directed workshops; but I have no record and cannot recover it now. What I have is random images of places I can't remember being.

Much is missing from any account. All I didn't see or know is missing. What I choose not to show is missing.

But come inside my head. Change has come, and trouble. I have been part of great change, or an echo of great change. I've been in migration, and watched migration pass me. I've been sheltered, not in or on the edge of great public change, yet cold and wet and in the dark, hearing the footsteps, seeing the fading dust cloud of diaspora, feeling at least a candle's worth of holocaust, hearing echoes, sensing reverberations, always sheltered and at a distance. No, not always.

Much is missing. Sometimes I don't know what to make of myself, yet there is no self but the self I make.

13

What Happens Then?

Time breaks. The landscape shifts. Identity fizzles out.

14

And Then What Happens?

Is it only *after*, I wonder, *after* great change that the need to know the name and look of things becomes urgent? Change seems to assault identity, to undo time, to devastate the landscape. Have the momentous changes of the twentieth century pitched us into a lasting nostalgia? Does the ache for home entail topophilia, a love for the place that never was? When we fall into history, must we spend at least a season aching for our house, our place, ourselves? After change, the losses mount. And when is *after*, and what comes next?

LATER

15

Counting the Losses

In the hot summer of 1980 I gave up gardening, but I remember working in the garden for years. I judge it's a good thing to do, even if the only regular produce is okra and black-eyed peas. Weeding between the rows kept me as often as not in a posture for prayer, which is convenient. I remember noticing one spring that the weeds were coming along especially well, remember deciding that I needed a new hoe.

Before I went to hunt for one, I browsed through the Sears catalog to check types and prices. Many as old as I am or older, and most younger than I am, have not been conditioned to the Sears catalog as I have been, and so may not understand how surprised I was to discover that there were no garden hoes in the new catalog. Some are available in the Sears store, to be sure, but not one was exhibited in the catalog. It was, for me, an astonishing discovery.

I did what I thought a proper scholar should do. I forgot the weeds. I neglected the garden. I got curious about the disappearance of garden hoes from the catalog, thinking that I had, perhaps, stumbled on something of sociological and cultural significance. I thought first that I had better check my memory of earlier catalogs. I went to our library, where, deep in the farthest recesses, there is a collection of Sears catalogs—not all of them by any means, but about one for each decade as a sample—and as good fortune would have it, I came upon a 1936 issue, particularly felicitous for testing my memory, for when it originally came out I would have been about to be seven years old, about to start the first grade.

Then, when I was young, the Sears catalog was a thing of great moment. Its arrival signaled the start of a new year—school would be opening soon. I never did learn how it happened, but word got around town quickly when the catalogs arrived at the post office just off the square. Once, I remember, my mother sent me to get it. When it was in my hands, I hadn't gone past Huls Drug Store toward home before I was in turmoil. One impulse was to sit down where I was, tear the wrapping off, and plunge in, but another impulse was to take it safely home, sit down, and savor it slowly, holding for last the pages where the toys were shown. The catalog was particularly captivating because I knew my mother would study it closely and then make a careful order of our clothes for the year and somehow sneak in an order for our Christmas presents without our knowing it. The book was also a resource for reading and drawing lessons, and in a rural community where flush toilets were rare, it eventually found other uses. Some families, I'm told, decided whether to do commerce with Sears or with Montgomery Ward by the quality of paper in the catalogs. The book is still important, for that matter: many of the appliances I have owned have come from the catalog or from the store after I studied the catalog, and sometimes, then and later, my mother told people that she got me from the Sears catalog.

At any rate, I still didn't get around to the garden hoe, thence to the weeds. Instead, I got caught up in the book and leafed slowly through it. The highest-priced dress was $7.98. An afternoon frock could be had for $1.98, a percale house dress for 49 ¢. Corsets ranged from 94 ¢ to $4.98, depending, I suppose, on how firm a foundation one could afford. Eleven pages showed different styles of long johns for men, ranging from 55¢ to $2.59. Men's shirts were available for $1.20, and separate dress collars were still exhibited at three for 60¢. Ten different kinds of wood-burning kitchen stoves were displayed against nine types of gas ranges. A complete living room outfit—sofa, two chairs, ottoman, table, and lamp—was priced at $58.95. School tablets could be had at two for 8¢. There were nine pages of patent medicines. The universal joint assembly for a Model-T Ford cost $1.45. There were eight pages of harness and gear. A good walking plow was available for $12.95. Three pages showed different styles of farm wagons. And sure enough, on page 908, there was a display of garden hoes.

The book showed a strange world, and yet it was less than my lifetime ago. Stunning changes have come since. That catalog showed another world; its features, design, style, and pace all foreign now, or quaint.

I have sometimes noticed change, sometimes not, have sometimes noticed while it was happening, have often noticed only later, much later. I have sometimes understood the consequence of change, sometimes not.

When my family moved away from the small town in West Texas to the big city in 1939, I didn't notice all that would mean, perhaps haven't yet, though I did know that I was sometimes unaccountably lonesome and miserable in the first months. Is it only after great change, and later, maybe much later, that we begin to know the consequence of change?

In the years after we moved, I think I must have gone back with my family a time or two, but gasoline rationing and tire rationing and the circumstances of the old family car were wonderfully dissuasive of travel. As best as I can recall, I went back only once in the 1950s, for Grandma's funeral, but as in the earlier return visits, I didn't look, or couldn't see.

And so it was twenty-five years after we moved away before I went back to look, hoping to see. By that time I had begun to understand that I was somehow longing for a place I didn't know and probably never had. I didn't know its roads or its contours, didn't know its birds, didn't know its trees, bushes, vines, wildflowers, weeds. I am reasonably adept at spotting sunflowers and fairly quick to recognize cotton when it's white in the field. Otherwise, I do not know the crops. I am caught away from that earth, whatever it may be, though I prize it. My father and his father once knew the risk of rain. They hurried the land with poor crops because they could not do otherwise, moved to town, got credit at the store, and I do not know their land. I do remember stories that my father told—how a bridge was built, how a certain horse ran, how he built a fire when the morning was cold, how farmers came to debt, how Uncle Jack used his broken fiddle as a whip, how Grandpa could lift a log three times his weight and raise a blister when the furrows weren't right, how my other grandpa's prayers could circumscribe Fate, and how even older men always called him Mister.

Eventually he came not to remember the stories he told me. Eventually I came to know that my memory affords only a partial and sometimes inaccurate record. I have wanted to believe that the truth about things is stored somewhere and might be found. Sometimes it is and can be; oftener, it's not and can't. After some years of searching, I learned that for the years I was most interested in, 1934–46, most issues of the *Jayton Chronicle* are gone. That was the weekly newspaper for the little town we left. About 670 editions were published in those years; about 240 of them survive. I cannot read the news in the missing papers. I am somehow an untidy file of time before; much is misfiled, and more is missing. The stories I think I know, I can't tell with much verve, for I expect that I've mostly got things wrong, or at least whomper-jawed.

When I had finished browsing in the 1936 catalog, I remembered where I had started, to get a new hoe to weed the garden. I took the 1936 catalog out to the big Sears store but was sorely disappointed: they wouldn't let me order a hoe out of the 1936 catalog. Since, I've come to suspect that even if I have a good hoe, I probably can't weed a 1936 garden.

Time passes and change comes, and it's mostly good. Indoor toilets are better than outhouses. Having a refrigerator is a helluva lot better than not having one. Being able to play a tape of Mozart's Third Violin Concerto whenever I want to beats being unaware that it exists. But change isn't always good and is seldom entirely good. When we were driven out of that place, we came to find others that were beautiful—Rotterdam and Heidelberg and the Blue Ridge Parkway and Charleston and the Palo Duro Canyon—but we were also hidden from good as we became fugitives and vagabonds. Change entails loss. Loss occurs in change. Sometimes we know it as it happens. Then, after and later, we see how much change has come and watch as the losses mount. "We know that we will lie down / in our own bodies," Mark Doty writes,

> . . . and someone will fold our hands
> and perhaps we will be moving
> although we are still. It might come true

of whatever we love or create
to replace what we love. There are buried cities,
one beneath the other. From the first loss, we begin naming.

I have sometimes — often, maybe always — thought that if I could just know things for sure, and say them, name them, then it would be all right and they wouldn't go away.

Some people seem to know for sure. Whatever is not theirs is not lost, only wrong or inconsequential. Good folk who may be otherwise altogether gentle and unassertive, when it is given to them to write reviews of restaurants for perfectly precious food sections in wonderfully knowledgeable magazines, begin to know without doubt that this sauce is bland, that too sharp, begin to know without doubt that the Belgian endives are imperfectly rendered, the snow peas ever so slightly out of place for correct presentation on the plate. They do not appear to grieve the loss of the contrary palate and sense that might have warned them toward other views. Experts seem to need to be experts, and we, unfortunately, ask them to be. In early spring to late summer the garden columnist in the local paper is not, I judge, paid to doubt his or her own advice: things are well in hand, recommendations are sure, and I guess we don't often wait to wonder what another adviser might have said. "Okra should be harvested every other day," one says, omitting to remember that if the garden is large enough, or small enough, it's nice and interesting to look every day. "Pod size will vary with variety," another offers, "but will generally be 4 to 6 inches long." True enough, but three-inch pods may be uncommonly tender and attractive and seven-inch pods may make good gumbo. "Test larger pods," another admonishes, "by cutting through them with the harvest knife." One would not, it goes without saying, think to approach a respectable okra plant with a disrespectable pocket Barlow, however sharp. Certainty is seldom certainty, though it seems so. I've sometimes wanted to know the precise right names for weeds and wildflowers and have imagined that I might learn them from those who are wiser and closer to the earth. I learn the names and then discover that three counties or three states away the precise right names shift away from me: there, the weeds and wildflowers go by other names, and I no longer know which plant we are talking about. But some seem certain. Writing about film adaptations of novels, John Updike remarks on "one of the charms of the authorial business—the text is always there, for the ideal reader to stumble upon, to enter, to reanimate. The text is almost infinitely patient, snugly gathering its dust on the shelf." He does not, I reckon, lose sureness, though I do, wondering whether a text does indeed wait quietly on the shelf. Some seem sure they know, and in their sureness seem not to miss what they might have learned by another kind of knowing. University administrators seem to know things and are sometimes patronizing of those—faculty members, say—who are not knowledgeable, not in on things. Though he does not seem to know much of anything unless it was filmed in the 1940s, Ronald Reagan was successful partly because he seemed to know.

Some know for sure. Some hope they know. The protagonist in Eric Larsen's *An American Memory* goes down toward madness as he searches obsessively for meaning in the life of his father, an angry intellectual and amateur photographer: "In spite of our better judgment and without hope of success," he says, "we find ourselves attempting to imagine, recapture, seize again the exact moment in abandoned, echoless, irretrievably lost time when the eye of the doomed photographer saw precisely what we now see." Some hope. Raymond Carver writes in "This Morning,"

> I had to will
> myself to see what I was seeing
> and nothing else. I had to tell myself *this* is what
> mattered, not the other. (And I did see it,
> for a minute or two!) For a minute or two
> it crowded out the usual musing on
> what was right, and what was wrong—duty,
> tender memories, thoughts of death, how I should treat
> with my former wife. All the things
> I hoped would go away this morning.
> The stuff I live with everyday. What
> I've trampled on in order to stay alive.

Some know for sure. Some hope they know. Some know they don't know. In "Citizen Mandel, Ph.D.," Oscar Mandel says,

> I cannot build the house where I'm alive,
> I do not understand the car I run.
> And when I flick my lamp don't ask me how
> A turbine wires me respectful light.

I have sometimes — often, maybe always — thought that if I could just know things for sure, and say them, name them, then it would be all right and they wouldn't go away. In my files I've kept a clipping from the *Fort Worth Star Telegram* for Friday, December 9, 1977. The headline says "Icy Arctic storm slices U.S. midsection," and the article reports on the weather in Texas (a fifty-degree drop in the afternoon on Thursday), the Dakotas, Michigan, Minnesota, Pennsylvania, Indiana, and Illinois (seven inches of new snow over most of that state). Cathy was in Evanston that year of the area's record snow. I had thought somehow that the article might let me know for sure how it was with her. In the same file there is a map of Evanston's Chicago Avenue and Main Street shopping district. I see there how we turned west off Chicago on Washington, then south on Custer, where her apartment was, but I don't know how the weather felt that winter.

From time to time I've tried to hold against change, to keep days against loss. I've been unfaithful in the effort where a successful effort wouldn't have worked either. In desk drawers and file drawers and on my worktable there are unkept journals in diverse shapes and colors. I meant to keep the days, but they are gone. One commences with August 11, 1967, and just thirty-eight pages later leaves off on September 4, 1973. Thirty-eight pages won't hold six years against loss. The entry for September 5, 1968, says, "The crape myrtle (it is East Indian — how did it come here?) is late in blooming, but lovely. The one on the nearside of the driveway is darker. This is the last day before the public schools open. I have not marked the end of summer except in my mind, as we all have. David's plan was to play 54 holes of golf. The weather may prevent him, but I know he is marking an end. Next summer will not be the same."

Except for some notes about work, a hiatus follows. The next entry is for August 1, 1970, when I apparently was seized, though not permanently, with record keeping. The August 1 entry shows that it was still 95 degrees at 8:00 P.M. The entry for the next day: "100 degrees at 3:45 P.M., but the unsheltered thermometer on the west wall of the garage, full in the sun, registered 116 degrees at the time." By August 5, 1970: "I don't even keep the temperature record very well." On August 7: "At 4:10 on the exposed thermometer, in direct sun, 117 degrees, 102 degrees on the other." By August 15: "At 7 P.M. exposed, 94 degrees. Yesterday it rained in Abilene, the first time in 73 days." August 19: "Rain, officially 0.48 inch, the first since June." August 20: "At 3:30 in direct sun, 119 degrees." August 25, 1970: "No record. Gone." September 1, 1970: "Gone."

Keeping notes is not the same as keeping time, but if you don't keep notes, nothing is left.

Another hiatus follows, then on February 1, 1971: "On Saturday (30 Jan.) we planted a tree, a non-bearing mulberry. All sighted and squinted to locate it well. When it was in the ground, Cathy stood in benediction and said, 'I pronounce you tree, in the name of Mama, Daddy, and the rest of the family.'" The March 1, 1971, entry reports that David and I put out onions. The March 6, 1971, entry tells that we planted a sweet gum tree (it died) and a redbud tree (it survives and thrives, yonder), and continues:

At dinner the phone rang for Mindy. As she was putting it down, it slipped, and the clatter caused my wife, whose back was turned, to think Mindy had hurriedly thrown it down. Mindy protested her innocence, remarking that her mother had "jumped to the wrong circumstance." A little later, still at table, I was asking questions, as we often do—this time about composers. Mindy, upon being asked Schubert's first name and not knowing it, answered "Lime." From that, we fell to talking of Cathy's piano lessons. David wondered if Cathy might someday want to teach piano, but she thought it impossible to work with kids. She had started Mindy on the piano early, and Mindy reported her prime directive: "WHEN

Another hiatus follows. Keeping notes is not the same as hold-ing time, but if you don't keep notes, what's left?

When the journal resumes, it's spring 1971, with reports of plantings—jalapeño peppers, banana peppers, cherry tomatoes, geraniums, verbena, onion, garlic, mint, radish, okra.

Silence again until spring 1972. On March 12, 1972: "Scarcely an inch of rain in the last four months. Today the buds on the mulberry began to open. The leaves inside are still folded tightly together. The pink buds on the apricot have in ten days given way to white flowers and then to green leaves pushing through the flowers, which now are falling away." Most entries for the spring tell of plantings—radishes, cantaloupe, crookneck squash, okra, onions, pinto beans, black-eyed peas, marigolds, lavender, rosemary, dill, sage, thyme, summer savory, marjoram, basil, zuc-chini. The entry for June 27, 1972, says "fence completed around back yard," and I wonder why I took so long to do it.

Silence again until the spring of 1973, with much planting in the expanded space: English peas, onions, rose bushes (mostly Mirandy and Peace), radishes, cabbage, tomato plants, corn, pinto beans, black-eyed peas, lettuce, zucchini, okra, turnips, cucum-bers, squash, zinnias, carrots, broccoli, mustard greens.

The journal ends there.

I left many blank spaces.

Apparently I decided to start fresh. The next journal is new. It has 124 pages. I used 8 of them. The rest are blank. Now it's the fall of 1973. David is in his third year at TCU. Cathy is beginning her first year. Mindy is a freshman in high school. Keeping notes is not the same as holding time. There is no holding time.

For eight pages, though, I did make almost daily entries:

Tuesday, August 28, 1973—When we came home from moving you into the dormitory, all of us were disjointed and lonesome. We brought barbecue in for supper because none of us wanted to do anything. I guess sometimes that left to my own impulses

I'd cripple you with hovering and keeping. But why can't we be together, all of us? I went to session meeting after you called, and was very Presbyterian. Home afterward, to read the paper, watch the news, and read. Your mother is near sleep. I wanted you to know what we were doing and where we were.

For the first few days, she'd be in and out of the house, back to the dormitory, and on.

Wednesday, August 29, 1973 — How long will I keep this up? Do we become used to sadness and accept it as normal? After I saw you this morning, I came home for lunch and had a peanut butter sandwich. Your mother had leftover barbecue. Tonight, salmon croquettes (that comes from French *croquer*, to crunch), cabbage, and black-eyed peas. I went to church for a meeting of the new teachers and the Christian Education Committee. We were very Presbyterian again, but not too educational. Mindy is invited to a 1950s sock hop at Colonial on Friday night. I've had more growing up to do this week than I can manage.

After that, the entries get shorter and shorter and more cryptic, and often I can't catch what words and phrases were supposed to hold in memory. I look at samples:

Tuesday, September 18, 1973 — David's birthday. Grand meal, with all about me. Chills.

Wednesday, September 19, 1973 — Quiet. Leftovers from David's dinner. Out for tobacco. Cathy's pictures, a smock. Donuts for Mindy's breakfast.

Saturday, September 22, 1973 — Fall officially here. All home, and yet a terrible cold at the thought of their going. Why does the night come?

Monday, September 24, 1973 — What have I thought? Creole zucchini and meat loaf.

Tuesday, September 25, 1973 — My birthday. Praise for great joy. Family all around me. Presents. Paints, pipe and pouch, *Mikado*. We listen.

Wednesday, September 26, 1973 — Rain, and the three out. When children grow up, they go out in the rain and get wet, and some-times you don't even know.

Thursday, September 27, 1973 — Quiet. Chills, Mindy practicing. David to class. Cathy gone.

Saturday, September 29, 1973 — Cathy's birthday. She is in College Station. First time any of them has been away on a birthday. Went by bus, a little apprehensive. Box for dogs. Mindy off to a party. David shouts "Go, Henry" for Aaron.

Sunday, September 30, 1973 — All safely home. Your mother is required to sit in the closet with Phantom while she has her kittens.

Monday, October 1, 1973 — Birthday dinner for Cathy. Roast beef and Yorkshire pudding. Cathy at the piano, then back to the dorm.

Sunday, October 14, 1973 — My father's birthday. To their house. Then we backed out of their driveway, they stood in the yard and waved.

Tuesday, October 23, 1973 — Mindy stood in the bathroom and tried to think her hair curly.

Thursday, October 25, 1973 — Troops alerted. All stunned. Cathy came home to ground. Rouladen.

Saturday, October 27, 1973 — Mindy's birthday. She to garage sale. Your mother worked at Octoberfest. You went, then home to rest, tired, sleepy. David at hours of horror movies. Dinner for Mindy.

Saturday, November 3, 1973 — Cloudy, dreary. To campus for mail about 5 P.M. Lonesome. Lonesome. Walks, trees, library, leaves.

Sunday, November 25, 1973 — This is the end of the Thanksgiving holiday. I have more than I can count to be thankful for. All here, all home. What of the bleakness?

The journal entries end there. The rest of the notebook is blank. Although I can't always reclaim what the notes signify, I'm glad I have them and the notes kept sporadically in the journals before and since. I'm glad I have them, but they don't reclaim the time. Keeping notes is not the same as holding time. Time passes. They go. They all go, and the losses mount. I have sometimes — often, maybe always — thought that if I could just know things for sure, and say them, name them, then it would be all right and they wouldn't go away.

Doesn't seem to work. Cathy is in Washington now. I have not seen her or talked to her in more than three years. I can't keep her time or tell her mine.

When would she cry, if she would cry, I wonder, and where? I guess she wouldn't. She was never much given to crying. I remember only twice. Once, when she was maybe fourteen or fifteen, tears rose with force that swept through her reserve, and she would accept no comfort. At first, I wondered why and may still not know.

She wept and paced a circle, dining room to breakfast room to hall to living room to dining room and around again and again, walking herself to control. I believe she thought that she should not cry.

Then later for Devola, her cat that lay upon her breast when she read or watched television, now dead in the street, her tears came hard, though she repressed them soon. I made a grave for Devola in the garden. I marked it with the cross of good plain wood that had held a politician's sign in our front yard, and wished I knew a spell against her grief, or any she might know.

And when would she cry now, if she would cry, and where, were she alone or scared or cold? Where would she cry? Find comfort? Ease? Not on my shoulder: I guess she couldn't.

16

Losing the Count

What happened just there? Just then? Did I know who I was then, before? Do I know now who I was then?

Seems unlikely: observation is always insufficient; memory is always wrong.

Why didn't I keep notes? More? Better?

I wonder why I have come sometimes to imagine that nothing is real until it's said, written—and then it's inadequate or worse because it rests on insufficient observation and errant memory. Perhaps I'm only your basic, maybe even prototypical (oh, I like to think at least that) post-Gutenberg man: nothing exists until it exists on the page.

I have the wrong questions. NOT: Why didn't I keep notes? More? Better? BUT: Why didn't I look more closely? Keep track? Pay attention?

If I didn't, and I didn't, is there any way of knowing who I became since, if observation is always already insufficient and memory is always already wrong?

I have imagined, or wanted to imagine, or believed I imagined that nothing related to me will count unless I get it outside myself. If what I think I observed or remembered becomes a piece of writing, then it's all right to consider, but not so if it's just myself. That's a strange disclaimer on myself, that nothing has value until it gets to be no longer myself. Strange disclaimer, impossible of fulfillment: whatever I observe or remember or say or write is always myself, whoever was, whoever is, even if some other witness transforms it.

But I can't easily rid myself of that urgency to abstract from myself, to find a large truth out there in the small particular I've known. Perhaps my little migration has been a version of the *volkswanderung*. Perhaps my losses do make a little holocaust. If there's any truth out there somewhere or in here, it's in the character of the small particulars, and I didn't keep notes enough, it may be, to tell for sure. How in the hell am I supposed to know what to make of all this if I didn't see it or, seeing, remember? If I don't know what I've left out?

Memory won't keep what we were, won't hold all the things that were in the world with us. Why didn't I look more closely? Keep track? Pay attention? Keep notes more and better?

17

The Snapshots I Have and the Snapshots I Don't Have

> I am
> paying attention to small beauties,
> whatever I have.
> —*Sharon Olds*

I can't keep them, hold them.

At the end of Larry McMurtry's novel *Leaving Cheyenne*, Johnny, the old cowhand, reminisces about his friend Gid, now dead, and Molly, the woman they both loved. In the closing lines of the novel he remembers a time when they were all young and he tricked Gid out of time alone with Molly: "So poor Gid got about twenty minutes. I guess it was kinda mean, really—nobody gets enough chances at the wild and sweet. But he would have done the same thing. There's just two things about it that I really regret. One was not being there to see the look on Gid's face when he heard that crippled mule clomping up, and the other is forgetting to bring a Kodak that morning, so I could have got a picture of Molly while she was sitting in her blue and white dress on the schoolhouse steps." In my younger days when I was wise, and maybe again not so long ago, I sometimes railed against those who were, I thought, obsessed with family photographs and home movies, like a youngish family I know—they take pictures of their child every month in the same setting and against the same props to record her growth. Better, I thought then, to watch, to look closely, to pay attention, than to run for a new roll of film. Scrapbooks and albums, I thought then and sometimes now, grow thick and bulge against their bindings with snapshots and letters and cards and ribbons and remain dear, but they lose their context and immediacy, lose somehow the warm impulse that gave purpose to our keeping snapshots and letters and cards and ribbons.

But what if you don't see? Or, having seen, can't remember?

I have wanted to hold moments, to mark the days, oh, to mark the days and keep them.

I have notes, journals. Some are undated, and I cannot quite place them.

I have wanted to hold moments, to mark the days, oh, to mark the days and keep them.

I can't keep them all in place and safe.

By the time he was seven, David had drawn a strike zone with chalk on the garage door. In the years that followed we acquired a series of solid rubber balls, each about the size of a baseball, and he wore them out. He was faithful. Later, he had uncommon control when he pitched.

For a long time, maybe when she was three and four and even five, Cathy kept little hard plastic dinosaurs, seven or eight of them, in what had been an Easter basket. She carried it about with her. The dinosaurs nestled in the artificial grass that came with the basket and the candy eggs. Sometimes she added real grass to supplement the artificial. Once, she took the leafy stalk ends that her mother had cut off celery and made a jungle for the dinosaurs in the basket.

I've been acquainted with dinosaurs. I'm a dinosaur.

I have a note that says only "Pie and Mrs. Prouse." Mrs. Prouse was Mindy's first-grade teacher. Otherwise, I can't catch what the note was supposed to help me remember.

Once, when Mindy was in the first grade, she left a note for her mother before she went off to school. I have it. It says,

Dear Mother Pes let
Leigh Come over to Day

PS PES!

We discovered stinging scorpions in the cabin we rented at Robber's Cave State Park in Oklahoma. For the rest of our stay, David dealt with the possibility of scorpions by being cool, Cathy by stomping instead of walking so as to mash any she might encounter, Mindy by never touching the floor. She leapt or climbed from bed to chair to chair.

I guess she was three. Unable to find her pajamas, Mindy came into the study where we were. She was wearing a white tam with red trim and a little red ball at the top. Nothing else. She was ready for her pajamas. I wish I had a snapshot.

The house on Bellaire Drive North is gone now, the whole block given to condominiums. It sat high above the street. The yard dropped from the porch in two stages. A catalpa tree stood in front of the porch but lower, below the first drop. By the street, below the second drop, there was a hackberry tree.

One August, before 1963. The catalpa leaves were beginning to curl and dry and drop. The tree somehow dropped beans beyond its branches. On past where Cathy wrote her name with chalk on the sidewalk stood the hackberry, mostly straight, still somehow mostly green. When I stood leaning against the porch post, what I could see of the campus across the street, where Cathy was playing, was framed and faceted. The catalpa beans hung, antique brown, cross-hatching the tiered branches. The hackberry greened the middle distance. I saw her in moments, caught by moments, framed by the vertical beans against the horizontal branches, running across the campus into a frame and then another and then at moments gone, running against the hay-pale August grass and the blue shadows of the silent halls. In one frame she'd sit, in another stoop and look. Then she was running again, her arms held out before her, her hands suppliant. She would tell me later, "I was going to help a robin. He was flying very low."

Well, I had a moment. I saw her through the trees, had a vision framed.

Then what lay nearer, the hackberry and the catalpa, found

and claimed my eyes. I stooped to gather beans that had fallen somehow beyond the branches of the catalpa tree.

He pitched until he was sixteen. In his last season, playing for the Crowley team, he pitched every game. By that time the asthma did not grip him so fiercely. When he was pitching in earlier years, especially in the later games when the pollen was high, sometimes I could hear him wheezing. Even then, the practice time he spent throwing against the garage door served him. He knew how to pitch.

Cathy was the first to be away from home for any length of time, that time she went with a church group to Mo Ranch, in the hill country near Kerrville. I vaguely remember the pool, the river, the dormitory, the catwalk, the chapel where she played the organ. When we went to get her, she had blisters on her feet and she was tired, but her jeans were looser, and she was aware, active, more knowing somehow than she had been. What had she seen, I wondered, that I had not? I wanted desperately to share in it, but then it would not have been hers. What had she learned, I wondered, that was not my teaching? I wanted desperately to know, but couldn't. What lovely mysteries did you see on long nights, strolling that high catwalk, that I've not seen? New stars? New powers? A waning moon? All far off?

We had made the reservations much earlier and felt a little obliged to go, and sort of wanted to go and didn't want to. The trip to Colorado, to South Fork, and then to Taos and Santa Fe, should have been a good one and mostly was, I guess, but we had all been caught up in the Watergate hearings and didn't much want to go off, though we did.

In his last season of pitching, before he gave up baseball to concentrate on golf, David pitched a no-hitter for the Crowley team. In the last inning, the third baseman bobbled a slow dribbler that let a runner get on first. Otherwise, no one else on the other team got that far. No one hit. No one walked. God, it was pretty.

When Mindy was maybe six and David was about twelve, he taught her all about golf. Cathy, who was about nine, didn't listen because she already understood such things. "Why do you have those little pointy things on the bottom of your shoes?" she asked him. She had already figured out that the sticks were to hit the ball with and the bag was to hold the sticks with. But she didn't know about the shoes. "Why do you have those pointy things on the bottom of your shoes?" she asked him. And so he told her.

Then one time when she was about twelve and he was about eighteen, she remembered to be indignant. "Do you know how long I believed what you told me about golf courses?" she asked her brother. "Do you know what he told me about golf courses when I was little?" she asked her mother. "Do you know what he told me about golf courses?" she asked me.

David said he guessed that he didn't know how long she believed it. Her mother confessed that she didn't know what he had told her about golf courses, and I allowed that I didn't know what he had told her about golf courses, though I assured her that I knew pretty much everything else.

"Well," she said, "he told me that they hunt places where there isn't any gravity to build golf courses and he told me that they find places without gravity so the little balls will fly farther, and that's why you have to have those pointy things on your shoes because since there isn't any gravity, you have to have something that will hold you on and if you didn't have the pointy things you would fall off, and I believed him for a long time."

Since, I have sometimes thought that maybe he was right after all, that maybe we've had it backward all these years, that maybe all these years we've been holding earth onto the bottoms of our feet.

Often, when all five of us were in the car and driving for any length of time, the girls would be seized with singing. They'd sing "Gaudeamus Igitur," hitting hard on "nos habemus humus." They'd maybe sing "Ash Grove." Then, Cathy doing alto, they'd sing a particularly slow and lugubrious "O Shenandoah," so David would cringe in the corner, and wind up, usually, with "Ninety-nine Bottles of Beer on the Wall."

I have a note that I scrawled for Mindy. Maybe it was during the summer after she finished high school. It reads:

> Mindy Sue Sweetheart
> — out shopping
> — back soon
> — be nice

Below my note she in turn left another:

> To Whom it May Concern Baby,
> — out shopping with Melanie, back by three

Then there is an arrow drawn to my last line, which is particularly scrawly, and she adds, " — I would, but I can't read your writing."

Another note, this from David, maybe during Christmas holidays while he was in college: "I've gone to Mountain Valley to play golf — left house about 11 o'clock." Below that he lists the whereabouts of the two cats, the two dogs, his two sisters, his mother, and his father. Then a final note: "11:05 I went outside and changed my mind. It's cold."

I remember the time Mindy invited us to a campus talent show at SMU. She was to do something — we didn't know what — with her sorority sisters. It turned out that the group did a medley from *Fiddler on the Roof*. When the curtain opened, there was Mindy, perched up on top of a stylized hut, playing the fiddler's theme. I wish I had a snapshot.

I have the program for services on Sunday, November 21, 1982, at the National Presbyterian Church, founded in 1795 as St. Andrew's Church. It was Saint Andrew's Day, and after the organ prelude there was a procession of the St. Andrew's Society, kilted, with pipes. Were we there, Cathy?

Once at dinner, Cathy announced that she had decided she wasn't going to die. "I'm going to be divinely assumpted," she said. We were walking together toward school. When it came time

for us to go separate ways, I said, "Have a nice day." "I would,"
she said, "if you didn't put it in the imperative mood."

"What's Mindy doing?" I asked.
"She's going to make a long dress," Cathy said.
"Oh. For her recital?"
"No, she's going to a dance."
"What dance? Nobody asked me."
"I didn't know you wanted to go," Mindy said.

"Some people," I was saying, "are impressed when they talk
to me."
"What did he say?" Mindy asked Cathy.
"I don't know," she said. "I wasn't listening."

Sometimes, when Cathy was in high school, we walked together
a way—out the back door, out the driveway, onto Devitt Street,
then left and north on Odessa Street, then east on Berry Street.
After one block on Berry Street, my way took me north on
Wabash toward the campus, while she went on east on Berry
Street. The corner where we parted is near the top of a long slope
up Berry Street toward us. That morning the sun was just up,
fresh and huge, at the far east end of Berry Street. When it was
time for me to turn onto Wabash Street, I stopped and watched
for a little while as Cathy went on east.
A miracle, maybe, occurred just then. She walked into the sun
and disappeared into its light and went on beyond my sight. I
turned north and moved on. I could not have a snapshot.

Undated notes, I think from 1973. I wonder what this list signi-
fies:

ice box
shed
lattice
lawn

space
inventions
miracles
painting

My notes show that it was 761.1 miles from home to South Fork, that time in 1973 when we went to South Fork, Colorado, instead of watching the Watergate hearings. And then through Slumgullion Pass, on to Lake City, and back. The notes show that we came back through Taos and Santa Fe and Cline's Corner to Fort Sumner and the grave of William H. Bonney, to Clovis and Lubbock, to Idalou and Lorenzo and Ralls and Cosbyton and down off the Caprock to Dickens and past Soldier Mound and Spur and Gilpin and Girard and Jayton and Swenson and Aspermont and finally home. My notes show 2017 miles, plus sketches of sand paintings.

Undated notes, still 1973. I wonder what the notes mean:

August — new year, old year for school teachers
depression, departure
August burns on my arms. I feel West Texas long ago, but it's all gone.
garden — prayer
why regret?
I regret the August sun.

And then Thursday, August 16:

Mindy: "A week from tomorrow I register."
Cathy: "A week from Monday I move."

And then Sunday, August 19: David stretched on the floor, watching television. Cathy curled in the yellow chair, reading, half watching television. Mindy on the telephone, leaning on the doorpost, watching. I might never see them all together like this again.

And then notes for Tuesday, August 21:

She will change
We will change

Each will do things the other will not know
We might even grow used to being apart.

Undated notes, I guess 1977. Yes, 1977.

Mindy: Box 1788
         Southern Methodist University
         Dallas, 75275

Cathy: 800 Custer Avenue
       Apt. 2C
       Evanston 60202
       (312) 864-2048

David: 295-7567
       1633 Westridge
       Cleburne 76042

Why can't I find notes that tell Cathy's address in Washington in
1982 and 1983? Mindy's addresses in Abilene and San Angelo for
the same time? Perhaps they're in the black journal: I won't look
there again.

Gregory Orr, in his poem "Near Dawn,"

> Come home, come home; I call
> my wandering ones
> back to my arms — out of dark
> out of storm out of endless harms.

   Music programs piled up through the years, none with snapshots, and I can't date all of them with any certainty: McLean
Middle School presents *Fiddler on the Roof*, probably in spring 1973,
and Mindy was in the orchestra; Paschal High School Presents
the Music Department in Concert, May 1, 1973, and I believe
Cathy was in the chorus; Paschal High School presents the Music
Department in Concert, May 7, 1974, and I guess by then Mindy
was in the orchestra; a string orchestra concert, undated, maybe
1976; a Youth Orchestra program for February 6, 1977, when they

played Beethoven's Sixth Symphony; others undated. The last one I have is the program for Cathy's organ recital on Friday, October 17, 1986. She played Larry King's "Fanfare to the Tongues of Fire," a Bach trio sonata, two Wagner transcriptions ("Liebestod," "Der Ritt der Walküren"), a Prokofiev toccata, William Bolcom's version of the gospel hymn "What a Friend We Have in Jesus," and the last movement of Vierne's Symphony no. 6 for organ.

I wasn't there.

They're gone, to Abilene or to Dallas or to Cleburne or to Evanston or to San Angelo or to Washington; gone, each in a nimbus of light.

Where are you going, child? Have I told you all I might?

I wish I could give you all you wished for, or might wish for.

Who will buy pens and pencils and paper for you?
It's the cold, maybe at twilight, or what Jay Parini calls

> the gilt-edged leaves
> that riffle in the slightest wind with that
> low rustling tinny note of early fall,
> the note of loss that makes me savor
> what befalls each step.

It's the cold, shuddering down my spine. I shake my shoulders to get loose, but I can't.

I kept wanting to mark the days, to make them special. All those days already were special, and I sometime didn't know. The time is gone. They're gone.

What if he called, needing me, just as I turned the corner? What if she called and I didn't hear? What if she waved as I turned away?

I can't keep them all in place and safe. Each is gone in a nimbus of light. They aren't mine to keep.

18

Already a Little Fuzzy
Around the Edges

I'd guess that it's best not to characterize oneself, whether by accident or by design, though it's not possible, I suppose, to live or talk without doing so. About some things, I think, a fellow ought to be reticent. Some qualities that we have, or think we have, or wish we had, ought to be discovered by others, not proclaimed by oneself: they may not be as evident to others as we think they are. Virtuousness, for example, or integrity or nobility or godliness, if they exist at all, probably ought to be found out about us by others, not self-declared. A fellow probably shouldn't call himself a poet unless others have already done so, and maybe not then.

Some characteristics and behaviors, I suppose, one might as well go on and announce. If you're about to proclaim truth about the national economy but don't know the gross national product, for example, or if you're about to lament the sorry state of geographical knowledge among high school students but don't know what teaching geography entails, you might as well admit it ahead of time: Folks will catch on pretty soon, anyway.

Best, in all circumstances, not to valorize oneself, though we already do so, by accident or design. I knew a lady once who could not invite people over without announcing that she had prepared "*my* nut bread" or "*my* apple pie" or "*my* chocolate cake," as if each were a national treasure instantly recognized by every eater. Each was good but not unique except in her annunciation. The nut bread tasted pretty much like nut bread, the apple pie like apple pie, the chocolate cake like what you'd expect. Not long ago I read a written version of oral histories in which various people recalled their experiences of World War II. One participant, who had been in combat for forty-two days, said he could remember every hour of those forty-two days. All honor to him, but he not only could not remember every hour of those forty-two days, he couldn't remember any single hour if asked to account for each moment, no more than any of us could. I knew a man once who established his own heroism through narratives of his day: "I really told him how the cow ate the cabbage," or "I told him this . . . and then I told him that . . . and then I really laid him out."

Most of us don't do so well. Mostly we're all there is, and nothing much — occasionally noble, sometimes mean.

Sometimes we make brave narratives of our day but long otherwise for the authority of unshakable ideas and unflappable leaders, surrendering ourselves to creeds we don't articulate, to heroes who don't come. Often as not, we're like Ruby, the speaker in Miller Williams's poem "Ruby Tells All":

> I wouldn't take crap off anybody
> if I just knew I was getting crap
> in time not to take it.

Sometimes we miss out altogether and begin to disappear.

Not long ago, I went as I often do to Frankelburgers, a hamburger place across the street from my office on the campus. I went to have a glass of wine and to read the paper. It was low time, sag time, mid-afternoon. Soon after I settled myself, an older gentleman came in. I'd often seen him there. By his years and his habits, I judged that he had retired; more than likely, I guessed, from a position of authority — his clothes were casual but fine, and he seemed easy in the world. He went to the counter, got a pitcher of beer and two glasses, and came to a table near me. He knew how to sit to beer and to table. He poured and sipped and waited easily, already companionable. Soon his friend, whom I had also seen often, came in and joined him. They seemed much alike in station.

"How many times have I been to this place?" the late man said.

"Some," the early man said, and poured beer for his friend.

"Walked right by it," the late man said. "Wasn't looking, I guess." He sipped a little beer. "Or maybe I'm old."

They sat awhile. They sipped a little. They looked out the big window. Maybe they saw far things.

"Holidays," the late man said.

"Yeah," the early man said. Thanksgiving would come on Thursday, and carols already crowded the air.

They sat awhile and sipped a little. They sat easily, I thought, to table and beer.

"What'd they decide?" the early man asked.

"We're going down there," the late man said. "Daughter, you know. Daughter, she wants to have Thanksgiving at home, at her own house, you know, wants her kids to enjoy it there."

"Same for me," the early man said.

"Going down Wednesday," the late man said.

"Yeah, that's when we're going out," the early man said.

They sat awhile and sipped a little and looked out the big window. Maybe they saw far things.

"Spent thirty years loading up every holiday," the late man said, "going to my folks' house, going to my wife's folks' house."

"Me too," the early man said.

"Looks like I'm going to spend the rest of my life loading up and going to my kid's house," the late man said.

"Way it goes," the early man said.

"When do we get our turn?" the late man asked.

"I guess we don't," the early man said.

"Shit," the late man said.

Sometimes we're nothing much. Sometimes we're mostly like Ruby. Sometimes we miss our turn altogether. Sometimes we don't know what we're like (was I possessive, overbearing, even ominous, or merely trivial?) and may, in Gregory Orr's words, "need our ignorance to keep us brave." Mostly, Horst Kruger writes, "no one is a hero until afterward," and likely not then. The world is unfixed, waits to be made tomorrow, and we find we can't save those we love, can't fix the world.

Though I've often, in former times thought I could, have often said that when I get big, I'll matter.

These latterly days, I think not. I may not become. I may not turn out.

I know there's hope in revision, but maybe not for me.

They out there revise the world frequently and plan, as they revise, to revise again. The house where we first lived in Fort Worth, at 3319 Bellaire Drive North, is gone and with it the houses along the whole block. They faced the campus. Now a block-long string of condominiums fills that space, but the condominiums won't last. They too will be revised. What once were pastures southwest of the city—empty stretches beyond the fences—are covered with concrete, streets, apartments, a large shopping mall, all built to be revised. I don't much think I'll make it.

Some revision is good. Some revision is bad. I don't think we can assume that it will be good, as the composition textbooks I've used at work seem to do. Revised, I might be worse. The movie theater across from campus where I sometimes took my children on Saturday afternoons has been revised into a ruin, empty for years for lack of clients and parking space. That's bad. I wish it were filled with us, with life. The creek below the Presbyterian church where we sometimes played on the day after school was out—near the picnic tables and the shelter—has been revised, they say beyond family use; is crowded now with what some call vagrants, some call derelicts, some call homosexuals, some call criminals. I don't know, but it's crowded now and not a sweet, quiet, empty place to play on the day after school is out. That's bad. The campus where I teach has been considerably revised since I came years ago. All the buildings are air-conditioned. That's good, especially here on the edge of the Great American Desert. The library is much larger, the space and the number of books have more than doubled. That's good. The area between Reed Hall, where my office is, and the administration building next door has been revised over the years until it's pleasant. When I look out my second-floor window now, I see low brick walls for sitting, shrubs, heavy wooden benches, tables. That's good. The man who owns the first stretch of the Croton Breaks right at the edge of Jayton has been busy with a bulldozer, scraping and leveling, changing, revising, even building a small dam to make a small pond for the livestock. I recognize nothing when I go back. That's bad for me: by revising, he has torn the canyons outside my knowledge and raped my care, though I do not doubt that it is good for him. The uncaring wind and water, at any rate, did not wait for either him or me, had revised the canyons before we knew, and will again.

The composition textbooks that I pick up and sometimes use consistently recommend and applaud revision, as I suppose they mostly should. They tell us to think and to scribble and to puzzle and to work toward a first draft and then to resee, rewrite, maybe any number of times, and after awhile to do a final draft, and that's good.

And maybe not. When we revise, are we growing toward ourselves, or toward some conventional expectation of what's right that we imagine exists out there? It's all right, once in a while, if not to say no, then to question common wisdom. Revision is not invariably good. Why would we suppose that revision is always good, or even possible? Perhaps I can guess. We always had the hope of getting it right, sometime. We always had the knowledge that we mostly don't.

The Croton Breaks were right enough when I first knew them. I wish they had stayed as I thought they were then.

But they had already and always been revised by the uncaring wind and water.

Might we take each other, and the other out there, without revision?

The first draft may be all I have.

Perhaps I don't have time for revision. Perhaps I won't live for revision. Perhaps I can't resee without being someone else. Probably I should. But maybe this is it. Maybe that's all there is. I'm here. This is it. This is what passes for thinking, for myself. Can I get a witness? I'm always to be revised, I know, but how can I be revised? I couldn't get it right the first time and couldn't resee to make a second draft. Others will revise if they please and catch what they thought I might have said.

Unrevised, I fail, of course, and get no credit in freshman composition, or in life.

And unrevised, I am revised anyway. I grow a little fuzzy around the edges, and may disappear altogether.

I may already have lost myself out there somewhere, may already have disappeared.

And why should that matter, if whole generations disappear elsewhere?

I had thought I was, or could be, in here, in what I said or did or believed of myself. Character, however, is imputed by interpreters; ethos is as much assigned as achieved. I thought I was being someone, and when I got big, I'd get it right; but while I thought I was being someone, I was sometimes being someone else. If I thought I was gentle, others found me arrogant. If I thought I was being a father, perhaps instead I hovered, possessive, authoritarian.

It's difficult to achieve character if it's always being something else. "For the most part," Paul Zweig writes, "we wade about in a debris of failed hopes." Sometimes convinced that actions of the mind are the only real actions, he continues, we come to the ultimate democracy, "for everyone, even the most spineless of us, has a mind. And so we are all real, and don't have to do anything strenuous to prove it." What he neglects to say is that if we do "anything strenuous" to prove that we are real, the reality we "prove" out there is likely to be different from the reality we thought we had in here. Wanting to win a radical individualism but yearning for reality and notice among the tribes of memory and community, we're sometimes startled by the character we achieve or the character assigned to us, both inner selves and outer lives being reordered so frequently that it's a little hard to keep track, as Jack Myers tells in his poem "Do You Know What I Mean":

> For the sake of argument
> let's say there are three of me:
> the one with the bummed-out body,
> the one who senses things are going badly,
> and the bright one who can't cope. That's me!
> Don't get me wrong. It's a family.
> For example, if #2 has a sexy dream,
> #1 may salivate. That leaves 3 free to feel guilty
> or write. Only sometimes in the face of authority
> 1 opens his mouth and 3 slips out "I hate your guts!"

Then 2 tries to get 3 to repent, but isn't smart enough
and then everyone feels like shit and gets a headache.

Some people, of course, resolutely believe, as I have wanted to
believe, that there is a resolute, identifiable self, if not apparent,
then waiting to be rediscovered. I've been pretty sure, at times,
that I exist, but as Max Apple remarks, "When one hesitates, when
one examines, he usually finds things a little unsatisfactory, even
himself."

Do you imagine that I have been telling the truth? What have
I left out? What have I changed in telling? Michael Wood says
that "modern styles are confessions of failure, point helplessly to
a world which, in the end, eludes the writer." The idea of the mot
juste, he goes on, "has died on us, because no words are entirely
right any more. It is not so much that words have failed as that
reality has come to refuse the names we used to give it."

I've just been invited to come to a neighboring university to
speak during an annual creative writing program. The friendly
voice on the telephone tells me that they'd like me to "do" the
essay—someone else, he says, will "do" the "creative" part. Suddenly I don't know what I'm for or which self is going to speak on
October 6.

In what was originally a speech given at the opening of the ex-
hibition "Anne Frank in the World, 1929–1945" in Berlin in April
1986, then an essay in the *New York Review of Books*, Harry Mulisch
discusses Anne Frank's place in Dutch literature "which is, actually, nonexistent": "Her book has been translated into fifty-one
languages and about sixteen million copies of it have been sold.
If one asks anyone in the world at large if he knows the name
of a Dutch writer the answer will be 'Anne Frank.' But in our
own literary annals, any second- or third-rate novelist, wholly
unknown abroad and hardly known at home, receives more notice
than Anne Frank." What she wrote, he says, is not considered
literature, but it is not trivial. Why is this, he asks, and what's
happening? Did she just tear off a chunk of reality and present it?
Mulisch tries to find a place, a category, for her work. It can't be

literature: "the aim of literature is not truth about the world. The truth always implies a lack of freedom: things are as they are. Yet in literature things also are what they are not." Things, of course, are as they are, and they're not what they seem, and they aren't as they are. Somehow, Mulisch continues, she has to do with reality, not with art, but then he questions himself: "Has she left us then no more than a human document? Was she then no more than a kind of intelligent journalist recording her own experience and thoughts? This too is not quite the case either." "The more I find out," Mulisch goes on, "the less I understand it."

My little grievances are nothing like her travail. My sadness is nothing like what she faced. My lamentations are nothing like the lamentations sweet earth has heard. And yet, having written, I too go away, if not to die, to disappear quietly — Have I told you any truth? Do you imagine that I have torn off a piece of reality to show you? Who were you? And who was I? Neither self might be interesting, except that things are as they are, and they're not what they seem, and they aren't as they are, except that every self abuts all selves, except that every self sometimes contracts into the puny, sometimes grows prodigiously to become *volkswanderung*, diaspora, holocaust; or maybe not. Maybe, truthful or not, whatever I am, this is all there is, and the best I can hope for is what any of us at last can hope for: I learn from Martin Gilbert's *The Holocaust: A History of the Jews in Europe during the Second World War* about the "injunction of the dean of Jewish historians, Simon Dubnow, whose dying words, after he had been shot during a raid on the Riga ghetto in December 1941 were 'Schreibt un farschreibt!'" I am nothing beside him, my little woes nothing beside all the others, my little sadness only a leisurely meditation beside what others have known. I cannot, I think, become wholly new. I'm still trying to make sense of what I was, or am. Wherever I am, I am not sufficient: I cannot achieve either universality or impersonality. I am here, telling a little truth, or not, looking as I am able to look, telling all I can, or not, altogether uncertain whether or not there is some hidden inner self not yet revealed, but waiting. I yearn to join you, be known to you, but I am alone.

I discover or create sharable experience, but it is always what *I* discover or create.

Can I get a witness? A witness to say I'm real? And what will you witness to, Witness? You can't catch me. I'm not here, but I will write and record, write and record: "the violin rises / above the alto, a shrieking sound," Gerald Stern writes, "we humans / shriek at the end, we want so much to be heard." Heard—that is, seen, known. Send word. Send notice. Send love; oh, and soon, please. Can I get a witness? Daughter, John Ditsky writes,

> when later
> on you share the house
> of time with only these chaste
> books for father, will
> it seem I ever was?

I fade. Do you imagine that I have told you a little truth, or know it myself? I fade. They go. They all go, or die, and I dwindle to nothing.

19

Bob Coluci Died Last Week, and I'm Still Counting

He died on Tuesday, August 16, 1988. I learned about it on
Thursday. We were not close, I guess. I saw him away from his
work only once, briefly, at a concert. I saw him just about every
two weeks at his work. He owned the little pipe shop downtown
on Houston Street where I got the coarse-cut burley that I smoke.
I had tried other pipe shops before I found his, but many—especially the precious little pipe shops in the big malls—are run by
young people who don't know much about tobacco. Bob kept the
coarse burley to use as a base in tobacco mixtures. I like it un-
adorned, and so went to see him just about every two weeks. He
kept two chairs out on the walk in front of his shop and often
sat there to watch the world. Usually when I got there he said,
"Hey, Jimmy."

He had come in from home that morning, they said, and had
breakfast at the usual place. They said he was opening the shop
when the heart attack killed him. His body was sent to York,
Maine, for burial.

I don't know that I grieved for him. I miss him. He was quick
and quirky and, I'd guess though I don't know, once in a while a
little rowdy when he was away from the shop. Early on, he began
to figure me out. Twice in my early visits he asked me why I
didn't park in the parking garage that was free to the customers
of the shops in the building. Twice I told him that I had parked
a couple of blocks away, up by Billy Miner's saloon. He looked at
his watch and said, "You always come in at about the same time—
you know, Jimmy boy, I believe you're going to stop in at Billy
Miner's. They'll be opening right about now." I allowed as how
they did make a good Bloody Mary for eleven in the morning.
"Well," he said, "it wouldn't be efficient to drive all the way down

here just to get one thing done." Pause. "Be wasteful if you didn't stop in."

I don't know that I grieved for him. I miss him. Very soon, I expect, I began to fret for myself: Where would I get my tobacco? Who would pay attention enough to stock what I needed?

When they go away or when they die, I don't know how much I grieve for them, how much I fret for myself. When they go away or when they die, I go too, am taken away, not a little piece at a time, but all at once a whole layer of myself peeled away, and the layers go and I become thinner and one day transparent and one day gone.

I go to little towns in the West not to find what remains but to look for what is gone, what might still be present as a vacuum. I make a little litany of loss and confusion and despair. How can I fix the world? I can't. I finger my fears and try to name them, try to count the losses, but I can't catch them all. Caught in dread, in melancholy and lonesomeness, even when there is no occasion, I feel a chill on my back, and not even the West Texas sun will warm me. "Hear, oh hear, the night bird call," the old refrain goes, "soon, oh soon, the dark must fall."

They're gone, or they're going. It passes. Everything passes. I dread loss, even when it is not real.

Gone or going? I don't know. This morning I read—a day late by the world, but early for me—in the *New York Times Book Review* that American fiction wanes. Bharati Mukherjee remarks there that "the problem appears to be that inside and outside America, 'American Fiction' has become synonymous with the mainstream, big-advance, well-promoted novel or story collection, and that American fiction—clever, mannered, brittle—has lost the power to transform the world's imagination." Later, she adds that American minimalist fiction "speaks in whispers to the initiated." Gone or going? Or waiting? I don't know.

But yes, gone. Grandpa Durham's house is gone from the rise westward above the highway and railroad track and trestle, and the track and trestle are gone, too; the rails to wherever, the ties and timbers to make fences and sheds and borders for flower beds. Gone, too, the house where we lived on the edge of Jayton, right by the first canyons, and gone the shape of the first canyons, bull-dozed to make a stock pond. And gone, too, 3319 Bellaire Drive North, where we lived, where condominiums now stand, and Fort Phantom Hill, near Abilene, where only foundation shapes and partial walls and stone chimneys mark the horizon, where time and fire took the rest.

Gone or going? Yes. Maybe. The heroes we thought we wanted or needed? Yes. Joe DiMaggio isn't on the cereal boxes I see at the grocery store. Not long ago, Reynolds Price asked after the absence of art celebrating great figures of our time. Where, he inquired, are the poems, paintings, hymns that keep Marie Curie and Albert Einstein in our minds; or Picasso, or Claus von Stauf-fenberg, or others? And what about our popular heroes, John and Robert Kennedy and Martin Luther King, Jr.?

> They are plainly honored in the national imagination—mil-lions of chromos in millions of homes attest to that, and a grotesque hunger for news of their survivors (no gobbet too small or rank) continues to gorge itself. They are of course the subject of numerous memoirs, biographies, films. But is their absence from serious imaginative art only another sign of the disastrous separation of cultured life from common life; or have good writers, painters, sculptors, and composers been sensitive and responsive for years to a rising wound that is only now being heard?—*There are no present heroes. Most dead ones were frauds.*

Things have changed around us, and we have changed; we have found no usable substitutes for traditional definitions of hero-ism: "The explanations, again, would be complex; but important among them are the growth of compassion for the poor and powerless (traditional heroes being mostly highborn and power-ful), the backwash of revulsion after the Great War at the patent stupidity and savagery of politicians and generals, and—crucial—the steady spread by press, radio, and now television of intimate information." Revelation of intimate information, of course, will undo just about all of us.

The list of heroes, at any rate, is always short.

Perhaps we grew a tad wiser and began to learn that the only heroism is what we can manage to give. Still, it's lonesome without Joe DiMaggio and Davy Crockett. Lee Iacocca just won't serve. Gone or going? I don't know. Perhaps. Have the painters abandoned us? Left us behind, alone and wondering? Roger Shattuck remarked some time ago that "since Cubism at least, most major artists, like Greta Garbo, want to be alone. Most spectators feel the challenge of this shift very deeply." And didn't notice, until after it was wide, "the gap between two modes of painting, one representing the visible world, the other discovering forms of inchoate meaning." We had long since grown used to linear perspective, chiaroscuro, and depth — oh yes, depth, not a flat canvas. The last time I saw what had been my grandpa's farm, three horses and a colt grazed around the barn and the rubble that was the house. When I had looked enough, I thought, I turned to go down the slope, past where the trestle had been, to the highway and my car, but I turned to look again. The colt had stepped up on the concrete slab that had been the back porch. Oh painter, how will you catch that golden pony except you open your canvas to the impossible deep space behind, catching the golden pony, casting improbable, palpable shadows toward me?

Gone, yes, surely gone, the song of Sioux, Crow, Zuni, Ojibway, Maya. Thomas E. Sanders, Prince Nippawanock, praises beauty that will endure

> as long as the grass shall grow, for the leaves of our literature rustle with the same freshness and truth that pervades the grass — that green hair Smohalla refused to cut because it was his mother's. And that literature not only will endure, it will grow until such time as the Transplant American can say the final lines of the Beautyway section of the Navaho Night Chant with the Native American and understand them because he has learned to mean them; then, and only then, will a collective unconscious create identity for *all* Americans, Native and Transplant alike.

> > As it used to be long ago, may I walk,
> > Happily may I walk,

Happily, with abundant clouds, may I walk,
Happily with abundant showers, may I walk,
Happily with abundant plants, may I walk,
Happily with a trail of pollen, may I walk,
Happily may I walk,
Being as it used to be long ago, may I walk,
May it be beautiful before me,
May it be beautiful behind me,
May it be beautiful below me,
May it be beautiful above me,
May it be beautiful all around me,
In beauty it is finished.

Perhaps. And where is the song the Comanches sang? Gone. We didn't take time to learn it, or even to hear it. The Lords of the Plains stopped white expansion in Texas for forty years, holding them back behind a line that ran roughly down the state through Fort Worth and Austin. But they were few, and when troops were again available for frontier service after the Civil War, the Comanches could not stay them. Caught in Palo Duro Canyon, they looked up to see Mackenzie's soldiers, and their time was over; and we never learned their song.

Did women go before they ever got here? No, they didn't vanish—we don't look. Perhaps we never wanted them to be real, and never got past our earlier definitions and relegations. We learned not to look, or if we looked, to see not women but what we had constructed—figurines, possessions, servants, goddesses, whores—as the *nature* of women, which dictated their function. Now, in the chummy complacency generated by the apparent and never more than partial achievement of equality, have we learned all over again not to look? Maybe. I have failed to look and have not seen. Somewhere in here, deeper than thought, below imagination, I expect that I am supposed to guard, to protect my lady, to loom tall as a hero before her, even while I know that I cannot finally support, secure, or save her. I am lonesome for what I am not, fretting for myself again, not thinking of her, or them.

What if they all go? What if I outlive everything I see, or think I see?

And what if it turns out that we're not brave enough, and lose what we long for? Not brave enough to taste each other, to tumble around and over and under each other, to eat and to lick and to enter and to surround each other? Oh, that time we planned a trip—"You," she said, "drive deep and all the way, and I'll come up," turning, erasing the last of any line that's left between us, "and I'll come down and down while you push up, and we'll go far, so far, in our diverse directions, until we meet in Salt Lake City; your brine," she says, "my sea, and then go on together." And oh, she dances. And oh, that time I read a poem that told about sweet fucking, only not, told how, just here, he wanted deepest penetration, wanted her legs drawn "as if for bicycling, up," required just so her total and complete, her absolute *submission*? "Why'd he say that?" I asked her. "Who thought up *submission*? I thought it otherwise." "Because," she said (straddles me, rises to me, says Come on in Sweet Baby, uses all her skin to get around me, climb all the way up me, wherever she happens to be, everywhere), "he's never met us." And oh, that time she shuddered on the table. And oh. Will we not be brave enough? After a night of "couch-dancing" in Houston—the ladies strip and writhe, the gentlemen watch—Keith McWalter speculated about the future: "sex will be readily available but safe, because there will be no touching, no intimacy of any kind. The women will be beautiful. The drinks will be expensive. And the gentlemen will not move." Fearful of plague or intimate encounter, will we learn to couple chastely, contractually, hygenically, touching fingers around a test tube? How much of our public preoccupation with sex is, after all, nostalgia, for what we might miss, for what we might lose, for what we are not? Yeats might say, but he died.

What if I outlive everything I see, or think I see?

Did knowledge go before it came? Is that gone, too? White Western males of a certain age seem to think so, especially if the loss they lament is the loss of geographical knowledge of historical lore or literary information, especially if it seems to have produced or to have come from white Western male culture, the world of our *fathers*. Perhaps it's gone or going. The freshmen in my writing classes sometimes convince me that it is so, and others besides William Bennett, Allan Bloom, and E. D. Hirsch, Jr., think it is so. In *Society and the Sacred, toward a Theology of Culture in Decline*, Langdon Gilkey remarks that

> an autumnal chill is in the air; its similarity to the chill in other periods of cultural decline is undeniable. One can point not only to vast shifts in geopolitical balances of power and influence but also to the apparent disintegration of our reigning contemporary ideologies (East and West alike). It is even more the sense—as the studies on science especially indicate—that the intellectual and spiritual heart of the culture, its confidence in science, technology and on expanding industrialism, has come upon difficult if not self-contradictory and self-destructive days, and that the culture as a whole is thus entering a "time of troubles" of very deep scope.

Perhaps. Perhaps not. And yet they may be right. Some changes bring good, but even good changes are accompanied by loss. In an electronic environment, tempos change, if nothing else, and changes in tempos are changes in living, in thinking. I'm not *always* on the side of the past. I don't believe that television, word processors, and computers are instruments of the devil. Some years ago I squared off against a word processor and lost, came to see its gifts, though it ate three papers, two desk blotters, and one necktie. I even enjoy most change: I like the coffee pot that keeps my coffee hot without my chopping wood and tending fire, and, if presented a choice between indoor and outdoor plumbing, I think only the innocent would have any trouble choosing.

The spectacle of rapid change—and what happens to us *after* great change and *later*—is at least interesting, if not sometimes devastating, to watch. Sometimes I can manage to enjoy it, though I imagine always that I see some cautionary signals. Most changes aren't pure. Even the best changes are mixed; all entail the loss of some former good. Sometimes, too, I think, we focus too exclusively on some single agent of change—the television set, the computer, information storage and retrieval. Rapid change has come before, and we have missed in our focus. We cite, rightly enough, the development of the printing press as the beginning of great change, but sometimes we forget to notice that nothing like mass communication was possible until expensive silk paper had been replaced by relatively inexpensive wood pulp paper, which is what really released the print explosion in the eighteenth century. Now, we sometimes neglect to notice that the computer is not uniquely responsible for the so-called information explosion of the late twentieth century.

In most of the past twenty years, about 40,000 books were published and more than 25,000 periodicals, and about 1,300 daily newspapers, and some 3,000 weekly newspapers. At the same time, in most of those years, about 7,000 radio stations and some 1,000 television stations were broadcasting, and in each year about 13,000 films (counting all kinds) were made. The computer alone is not responsible for the explosion we see and hear. Electric typewriters have done their part. And photocopying machines. If earth reels out of orbit someday in a science fiction disaster, it may be because we made too many copies and tilted the weight too far.

Still, technological progress for many chiefly means improving computer technology and corollary electronic communication systems. Where rapid development does not yet reach, it is longed for as the signal of civilization, the right path for aspiration, the mark of superiority. All ages, to be sure, are technological ages in one way or another, but in former times technology commonly moved a little more slowly so that it was possible for us to accumulate its appurtenances gradually. The tools of the farmer and the accountant in 1890 were not all that different from those in 1840 or 1790. Modern technology, however, doesn't offer us a tool at a time to adjust to slowly; whole systems of method open up between the time we leave off schooling in June and take up working in September. Our way is technological and rapid, and we take that as appropriate, even if it isn't always.

Increasingly sophisticated technology, I'd guess, is not an unmixed blessing. Tempos change, and lives change, and modes of thought and performance change.

The typewriter is undoubtedly a blessing, but it may be responsible for a general shortening of our sentences, while a quill pen might have encouraged slow meditation prior to writing, longer sentence building in the head, and sonorities that we seldom hear now. Perhaps we pause longer with some tools than with others. If your word processor lets you revise readily, are you likelier to put down any old thing the first time? Does your fountain pen want you to think a while first? I don't know. Certainly we don't whirl electronically—amid optical fibers folded into a telephone line to carry phone messages, television, linkages to central information bank, amid a hundred TV channels, two-way cable TV, home video recorders, video disk players, portable video cameras, eyeglasses that also carry the news, amid all these and more, with earphones on our heads—without confusion. If one sends a message by telephone that results in hard copy at the other end, is it telephone service or mail service? Not long ago, the Federal Communications Commission and the Postal Rates Commission sued each other to find out.

Part of what made the information explosion an explosion was the miniaturization made possible by high-reduction photography, giving us first microfilm, then microfiche, then supermicrofiche, then ultramicrofiche, which made it possible to put up to thirty-two hundred pages on a single film not much bigger than a large postage stamp. That's roughly seven to ten fair-sized books. Meanwhile, high-reduction photography also made it possible to store representations of about eight thousand paintings on a single disk.

The technology already exists, though it is not universally accessible, to form sprawling electronic networks offering electronic plenitude to any computer screen. One day soon, students anywhere will be able to search the Library of Congress or the British Museum from their own local desks. Such long-distance searching may not even be necessary. With miniaturization, perhaps *any* library can house *all* libraries. Does that change the nature of the world? Or of how we learn it?

If students' consoles connect them to the world's entire resources, how are they to go about their study? How are they to choose? Where are they to start? Where can they possibly stop? Can they study these resources in the same way they would if they held book or journal in hand?

By their size and nature, books and journals invite readers to pause, to reread, to look ahead, to ponder, to look back; a terminal hitched to all of the world's resources invites readers to keep going, as fast as possible, for there is always more to come. Does one kind of study entail the same kind of thinking that the other kind does? Probably not.

No one would have to be taught to be grateful for the bounty that may come. Any school, perhaps, any little town, can have a great library and, with those video disks, a passable museum. But the machine giveth, and the machine also taketh away. Bounty can, in no time at all, seem like hopeless clutter. The machine brings speed, accuracy, reduced drudgery, efficiency, plenitude — and may rob us of the pause essential to that old goal, the examined life.

All of our forms of criticism, judgment, evaluation, and theorizing rest on our ability and willingness to pause. None is possible without meditative pause. But electronic devices promise speed, near-simultaneous answers to our questions, and — with the aid of high-reduction photography — a perpetual openness to a multitude of experiences. Electronic devices will not become more primitive. They will become more sophisticated and more accessible, provided that electricity keeps coming to the plugs in our walls. I don't know that they will make us better. I don't know that they will make us worse. I expect that we will learn to be different. The recent forms — movies, television, ultramicrofiche — don't encourage the same kind of meditative pause that we have hoped for. Of course, when you use a movieola you can study a film frame by frame, but when you do that you're no longer studying motion pictures. Print allows us to turn backward or forward, to stop, to finger, to reread. The nature of electronic communication devices is to move, to keep going, to hurry on.

That old goal, the examined life, demands that we pause. We haven't become especially wonderful in pursuit of that goal, though we're about the most delightful thing there is. Going into the future means becoming something other than what we are now, perhaps something quite unlike ourselves. Which beast goes toward which Jerusalem?

Shall we become new? Shall I outlive everything I see? Or think I see? I expect so, but probably not just yet. We still talk to each other in the same ways, and sometimes go to war. We haven't yet learned new rhetorics; don't entirely know how to take messages that are partly verbal, partly visual; don't quite know whether or not miniaturization and electronic communication have bred or will breed a new kind of literacy; don't yet know what to make of apparent shifts in our conception of knowledge itself.

Rapid change — and what happens *after* great change and *later* — is always at least interesting, if not sometimes devastating, to watch. We don't always notice change, even profound change. Perhaps we haven't altogether seen the shifts in what we think knowledge is, in what it means to learn something and to write about it.

For a long time we have supposed that knowledge is "out there," determinate, arranged in rankable parts, and we have supposed that we can individually "acquire" knowledge. Most educational systems, most teachers, and most students still operate according to this conception, whether knowingly or not. We organize ourselves — and knowledge — into discrete parts. We give tests that invite students, as Ronald Schroeder puts it, to regard knowledge as a "collection of inert, discrete parts." "Objective" tests, then, are the appropriate way to measure knowledge. All the "right" answers must be the same, for we have been supposing, Schroeder says, that knowledge is "abstract, impersonal, universally acknowledged": "'objective' carries with it all the implications of truth, legitimacy, impersonality, and universality. Something objective can be verified; personal idiosyncracy and prejudice do not affect (modify or even falsify) its truth. An essay, on the other hand, implies the subjective, and hence something limited in validity, authority, and truth by the peculiarities of its context." If we imagine that a thing known has an independent and separate existence outside its unique relation with the knower, then, as Schroeder says, knowledge is a "material quantity, independent of the knower," and we don't have to accept the responsibility for "creating the form that makes knowledge intelligible and meaningful."

What we have not yet done, Kenneth Bruffee suggests is "to explore the implication of the irreversible revolution in our conception of knowledge accomplished by Einstein, Heisenberg, and Goedel." When Einstein temporalized space and obliterated conventional fixed points of reference, showing that measurement is relative, his demonstration "dealt the first crippling blow to the hierarchical, determinate view of knowledge." The second blow was Heisenberg's uncertainty principle, which stated that we can never see things as they are when we are not watching them. "By virtue of our watching presence, things change their nature." Then Goedel taught us that there is no frame of reference that is self-guaranteeing.

When knowledge is made, not given—in here, not out there—then we can't go to the bank and draw it out. We are responsible for its keeping.

If our old rhetorics, our old ways of telling ourselves to ourselves and to others, were built within an old conception of knowledge, and if that conception has given way to a new one, then where are our new rhetorics? Not here, perhaps, not just yet. The old rhetorics sometimes served us well, but we never persuaded ourselves to study war no more, never learned to say *love* and *generosity* so that they might be realized. We won't get a new rhetoric until there is a new kind of creature. Which beast goes toward which Jerusalem?

And along the way, with such possible losses and some possible gains, along the way while I wasn't watching, did the culture die? The culture I thought I belonged to, maybe did, maybe didn't? Did everything go? Is everything going? Shall I outlive everything I thought I saw? I can't count the losses, don't know the gains. Worlds have already gone. Hopalong Cassidy won't come back.

In *Goodbye to a River* John Graves writes about whatever it is and wherever it is we came from:

If a man couldn't escape what he came from, we would most of us still be peasants in Old World hovels. But if, having escaped or not, he wants in some way to know himself, define himself, and tries to do it without taking into account the thing he came from, he is writing without any ink in his pen. The provincial who cultivates only his roots is in peril, potato-like, of becoming more root than plant. The man who cuts his roots away and denies that they were ever connected with him withers into half a man. . . . It's not that necessary to like being a Texan, or a Midwesterner, or a Jew, or an Andalusian, or a Negro, or a hybrid child of the international rich. It is, I think, necessary to know in that crystal chamber of the mind where one speaks straight to oneself that one is or was that thing, and for any understanding of the human condition it's probably necessary to know a little about what the thing consists of.

Did the culture I thought I belonged to, and maybe did, and maybe didn't, did that culture die? Some say yes. Some say no. Some don't notice. If it died, when did it die? Some say it died about the time the frontier closed. Some say it was in 1914. Some say in the 1930s. Some don't notice. I know that I never measured up to what I imagined its ideals were, and now I never can.

Some call it WASP culture, but that's insufficient. And peculiar. My friend wonders why we put the *W* there. "Did you ever," he asks, "see an Anglo-Saxon who wasn't white?" Redundant, he says. Better, he says, to leave it off. "That way," he says, "we'd get a better acronym—ASP is more lethal than the lowly WASP." I see his thinking, I believe, but I guess I'll disagree. ASP won't do. I'm afraid of snakes in general, but the asp always seemed in my mind to be especially quick, deadly, and precise. Anglo-Saxon males are responsible for most of what I hold dear, but when they have been deadly and destructive, they mostly haven't been quick and precise. They're more like what my mother used to say. "You're just like a bull in a china shop," she'd say to me, but then she'd add the second part that we mostly forget: "What you don't tear up, you shit on." I'll stick with WASP, not because it's best but because it's habitual, and maybe only modify it to Male WASP.

Writing some years ago about what he called "the decline of

WASP literature in America," David H. Stewart remarked that "for generations, the WASP broke trail for westering mankind." "WASPism," he said, "means a cultural heritage, not genealogy, ethnic origin, or race," and its two-sided, fierce religious zeal going "hand in hand with the old Anglo-Saxon love of land and plunder," and managing all the while to pledge the right of dissent as part of its affirmation: "The cultural environment within which the most violent dissenters' protest remains a WASP environment which determines the mode even of rebellion against it." The American WASP, Stewart said, was "evangelical by heritage, rural by necessity, and independent by choice." Citing expressions of loss in Hemingway, Faulkner, and Marquand, Stewart said that "such passages (and they could be multiplied to include most of the writers of that last WASP generation) may well signify the end of WASPism itself as an articulate force. It died." And with it "an entire complex of cultural values, a cast of mind." The old life survives, Stewart added, "in isolated pockets where people go on venerating the old gods" — or, he couldn't have known when he wrote, in the White House of the 1980s, where Reagan venerated not the old gods but movie versions of the old gods. WASPs made a hard, long run out of northern Europe all those centuries ago, and westward, carrying all the way a "power of blackness," in some part out of what would be Calvinism, in some part out of "the dark dreams engendered in the dark forests of northern Europe." They made a hard, long run, and now maybe it's over.

I never measured up, and now I can't, and Hoppy won't be back to help.

They're gone, or they're going. It passes. Everything passes. They die.

After great change, and *later*, do we dwindle, "Someone who is about to be left alone / Again, and can no longer stand it"?

What if they *all* go? What if I outlive everything I see, or think I see?

They made a long, hard run for the better part of fifteen centuries, down out of the dark in northern Europe and westerly. What did it come to? To Ronald Reagan, pledging allegiance to the movie version of what we wanted to imagine we thought we were? How many times are we removed from anything that might be real? Telling movie events as if they were actual records of heroism? Yearning to be John Wayne, to be an imitation of an imitation of an imitation? Worse comes.

When was it over? When did the culture die, if it died? Some don't notice. I think it was in the forty years or so after 1945, when the heart—rightly enough—almost went out of us. Did we finally see that we had killed too many; did we finally know that we hadn't turned out to be who we thought we were?

Our wars were righteous, of course, and we killed too many. But we didn't have to have war so that we could kill; some who shared our blood and, over time, some of our beliefs killed six million or so people because they weren't Western.

Occasionally someone objects that we focus too narrowly on the Holocaust, on the murder of six million Jews, that we neglect to remember and to mourn, say, the twelve million Russians who died in World War II. It's true that we don't remember and mourn. They were at war, we tell ourselves, and civilians die, too, in war, and besides, they were those funny-looking Slavs with high cheekbones and a strange alphabet. They didn't come into our consciousness. The six million came into Western consciousness, and died *because* they did so.

In her poem "Wherever We're Not," Shirley Kaufman writes,

> Home we keep saying, the keys in our pocket,
> as if there's a refuge
> nothing can change.

But there was no refuge, no home. Ordinary comforts disappeared. In a review of George Steiner's *The Portage to San Cristobal of A.H.*, Ronald Reed says: "How does one watch a child grow, share a friendly glass of wine, read a book in light of the concentration camp? How does one issue a prayer for the dead when there are six million dead?"

"The story is told," Lucy S. Dawidowicz writes, "that when the German police forces entered the Latvian Riga ghetto in December 1941 to round up the old and sick Jews, the Jewish historian Simon Dubnow called out as he was being taken away: 'Brothers,

write down everything you see and hear. Keep a record of it all.'"
Many did: I think of the diaries of Emmanuel Ringelblum and
Chaim Kaplan, and the work of Shimon Huberband, written in
Yiddish and hidden with the Ringelblum archives in milk cans
under a building at 68 Novolipki Street in Warsaw. Elie Wiesel
describes his methodology: "To look at small villages, at forsaken
communities: that lay far away from the centers. Names, names:
His aim is to redeem names; names of communities and names
of individuals. Who was shot where, who was hanged where."
Record everything, Dubnow told them, preserve everything, describe everything. The universe rapidly shrank and burned, and
yet, as Wiesel puts it, "independently of one another, without
contact, they found the strength and the faith to write, to leave a
few traces among the ashes."

Sometimes neither trace nor ash remains. Horst Kruger tells of
going back after long years to Berlin, among other things to see
his sister's grave, only to learn that the plot of ground had been
resold for another grave, because "earth is in such short supply":

> Just leveled it, just laid someone else in it—imagine some-
> thing like that being allowed. They can't take our dead away
> from us too, can they? I always thought to myself, The ceme-
> tery, there's time for that, it won't run away. Now I am told
> the grave no longer exists; my sister has been wiped out of
> the world, and to be fair, I am the one who killed her. So that
> is guilt; now I know how it feels. I have destroyed her grave—
> an ancient taboo, of course, like incest or matricide. Now it
> awakens, the ancient guilt. Nothing is left of her—she lives
> only in me. In me it all comes together. If I do not remember
> now, she will be dead forever. So I will have to remember.

Do you wish not to be blamed for what others did, wish not
to be taken as a participant in tribal crimes? Very well, disavow
the crimes, but disavow, too, tribal achievements; say, for a small
sample, the work of Samuel Johnson and Jonathan Swift and
Wolfgang Mozart and Thomas Jefferson, and, say, the Constitution of the United States and Edward Hopper's paintings.

We killed too many. We found we couldn't triumph simply by declaring the virtue of our identity and presence.

They made a long, hard run, a good run, those tribes.

Is this what it came to? Did it end against a black marble wall in Washington, D.C., where some came to note and to mourn individual souls, where all the other thousands of us came to mourn our culture, came to grieve that we didn't turn out to be who we thought we were? Oh, let us grieve that we died, or turned out to be trivial.

Gone? Are they gone? The novelists and the heroes and the painters? The women, gone before they got here? Is knowledge or the hope for knowledge gone? Is our way of talking gone, our hope for meditation, our chance to be still? Is that culture gone?

Yes?

I don't know.

But the people die.

Today is Monday, September 12, 1988. My mother's funeral was this afternoon. She died in her sleep sometime during the night of Friday, September 9, to Saturday, September 10; peacefully, I believe, if I can judge by her face when my sister and I saw her early on Saturday morning. I believe she had belief enough for herself and my father, though not perhaps for me. May Ruth Corder rest from her labors.

She was already long since lonesome for my father. He had already wandered away in his mind for two years before he died on May 15, 1988. His funeral was on May 18, 1988. He wanted to be a doorkeeper in the House of his Lord and never knew that he counted; and maybe he didn't in the world's ways, but I believe he had belief enough for himself and my mother, though perhaps not for me. May Nolan Corder rest from his labors.

The books I have studied bear no testimony to such quiet lives as theirs. Inside their heads, I think, life was not quiet, but I believe they believed enough to find their rest.

Have I already known the day of wrath, "the day that shall reduce the world to ashes"? I wish someone could or would tell me it is so, that wrath has come and may withdraw.

I can't say grace, can't say "God bless them all," or "may God bless them all," can't make a prayer to serve them all—such effrontery that would be, and why should I be permitted?—can't compose the Mass to tune them all toward Heaven, can't hold a wake, sit shiva for the whole world: I'm grieving for myself. What if I outlive everyone, everything I see, or think I see?

I can't sing praise. I am not a psalmist, not a priest, not a rabbi, not a preacher, not a prophet.

I can't write epic or tragedy or romance or adventure. Were I able, those lustrous forms would not admit, could never hold, the people whose names I yearn to celebrate.

Then how can I go on? I can't commence with "I thank"–such unmitigated gall, my mother would have said, such gall unmitigated in such a subject put with such a verb.

I can't say "bless them," or "God bless them," or "may God bless them," or "I hope that God will bless them." I'm not allowed; or allowed, not able.

One morning I said to my daughter, "Have a nice day." She said, "I would, if you didn't put it in the imperative." Later, maybe months later, I mentioned that all prayers seemed to be in the imperative: "Give us this day . . . , forgive us our debts . . ." "Yes, daddy," she said, "but the supersegmental phonemes change it to supplication."

But I can't know I have tone, pitch, and stress—those supersegmented phonemes—tuned to heaven.

I cannot sing "eternal rest grant unto them, O Lord, and let perpetual light shine upon them."

Then what? Not "remember the names." Perhaps "I hope that someone will remember the names." Perhaps "they lived," or "they live."

Ruth Corder lived elsewhere and then in Fort Worth, Texas, from 1905 until 1988.

Nolan Corder lived elsewhere and then in Fort Worth, Texas, from 1907 until 1988.

Bob Coluci lived somewhere and then in Fort Worth, Texas, until 1988.

The members of the third-grade class of 1938–39 at the Jayton school lived in Jayton and out in Kent County. I don't know who lives, who doesn't, or where. They live or lived, in alphabetical order, boys first according to the protocol of the time: Jimmie Wayne Corder, James E. Cox, Coleman Gallagher, Jr., Robert Howell (listed out of order in the book), Bobby E. Hamilton, Joe Don Jones, Hanford Long, Jimmie Matthews, Don W. Patton, Travis Earl Self, Bobby Ray Stanley, Billy Glenn Vencil, and, added later from diverse venues, A. J. Bruce, Nolan Grice, Alva Ray Mixon, Jerry Daniels, Earl Dean Rackley, Billie E. Nowell, Doyl Lee McCurry, and Aubrey Hatfield; then the girls: Lois Dean Bice, Leona Boling, Maude Adele Brown, Bessie M. Cross, Olive Engledow, Bobby Nell Fuller, Mary Jo Hays, Margie Lou Myrick, Lucille Robinson, Peggy Sue Robinson, Artie Grace Sanders, Cherrie Stanley, Leona Thompson, and, added later, Thelma Grice, Angela Andrade, and Linnie Fay Smith.

Sue Kinney was their teacher. She graduated from Sul Ross State Teachers' College, perhaps just the year before. Her salary was $73.13 per month. She was beautiful.

Nell Durham Poteet lived near Gilpin and in Spur and in Ralls and I don't know where else and died in Levelland. She was beautiful.

No one I know is left in Jayton or Spur or near. They have gone and left the town to strangers. Kent County and Stonewall County and Dickens County are emptied of my folk, and the places where they were will know them no more. They left sometimes in glad dispersion, sometimes in the face of tribal ruin.

Bertha Durham lived. She died somewhere near Lubbock. I don't know where. I don't know when, maybe 1960. I don't know what her name was before she married my uncle. Her eyes were big and brown. She was beautiful. She died of a sandstorm in her belly.

They, the dead and the living, suppose that I never think of them, but I hear them in my head all the time. Is it true, as Jeffrey Harrison says, that "the dead are all / just names now, the separation final"? I think I hear the dead — and the living, now gone. How can I make a litany?

Samuel Ross lived in New York and Iowa and diverse places and died. As I read Hamersly's *Complete Army Register*, he enlisted as a private in Company A of the Eighth Infantry on December 14, 1837, became a corporal on February 14, 1838, and a sergeant on June 24, 1839, an uncommon rise in an army slow to promote. He was discharged on December 13, 1840. He reenlisted as a private in the Second Artillery on March 6, 1841, became a corporal on December 9, 1841, a sergeant on April 1, 1842, and first sergeant on August 1, 1843. He was discharged on March 6, 1846. He reenlisted as a private in the Fifteenth Infantry on November 7, 1846, became a corporal on December 1, 1846, and first sergeant on April 27, 1847. By June 28, 1848, he was brevet second lieutenant in the Third Infantry. He resigned on May 30, 1849. I know no more of him until May 14, 1861 (I wonder where he was), when he showed up as a captain in the Fourteenth Infantry, brevet major on May 3, 1863, for gallant and meritorious service in the Battle of Chancellorsville, brevet lieutenant colonel on December 13, 1864, for gallant and meritorious service during the Atlanta and Savannah campaigns, brevet colonel on March 13, 1865, for gallantry and ability as brigade commander in the Savannah campaign, brevet brigadier general on April 13, 1865, for gallant service in the campaign against Atlanta. He was mustered out on June 13, 1865, but then reappeared as a major in the Twenty-eighth Infantry. He was mustered out on January 1, 1871, but then reappeared as a second lieutenant in the Seventh Infantry. Not long after, he retired as a brigadier general. I don't know whether or not he was beautiful, but he must have been interesting.

And there are silent thousands I can't hear—say, the Jews walking westward out of Russia after 1880, by paths I don't know. I hear only their footfalls.

How many times can you be a pallbearer without disappearing, whole versions of yourself peeled away in each death?

Silent, or near silent, all those young men who died in war but innocent of war, from 1861 to 1865. One young private wrote home after his first combat that in pictures of battle he had seen, "they would all be in line, all standing in a nice level field fighting, a number of ladies taking care of the wounded, & c & c but it isent so." In their innocence, Gerald F. Linderman writes, they were "confident that courage alone would see them through," but "one of Sherman's men wondered if God even knew who among the dead were courageous and who were cowardly."

Silent, or near silent, all those men, near half a million, who died in a year's fighting at Verdun. "Having despaired of living amid such horror," one Dubrulle wrote, "we begged God not to have us killed — the transition is too atrocious — but just to let us be dead." Marc Boasson wrote home: "I have changed terribly. I did not want to tell you anything of the horrible lassitude which the war has engendered in me, but you force me to it. I feel myself crushed . . . I am a flattened man." Lieutenant Jabert wrote: "They will not be able to make us do it again another day; that would be to misconstrue the price of our effort. They will have to resort to those who have not lived out these days." When it was over, the slopes of Mort Homme were a desert: "The Wind whistles through the trees and the birds sing, and that is all."

I know a small house, more accurately a small ruin, where the wind sighs and keens. When I saw it last, the walls still stood, and part of a rotting roof was there, from it protruding part of a rusty stovepipe. Even if I gave specific directions you wouldn't find it. You'd have to go west from Fort Worth, Texas, about 220 miles, through Weatherford, Mineral Wells, Breckenridge, Albany, Stamford, Aspermont, Swenson, on to Jayton, and by now you'd be in territory where it costs about fourteen dollars to send a letter to the world, but you'd not be there yet. Jayton, with a population of about 650, is the last big city before you get there. You'd drive about 3 miles north out of Jayton, turn onto a dirt road, and drive down deep into the Croton Breaks, and after a while you'd come close to what once was a little community known as Golden Pond, no longer recognizable as a community. The only inhabitants are ghosts, and the wind moans through the fallen planks of an occasional ruined shack. The little house was not far away. Made of native stone, it measured maybe ten feet by twelve feet, with a smaller wooden lean-to on the back. If you stand there even in bright daylight, in every direction you look the distance is blue and far and melancholy. It is the lonesomest country I know. If you stand there at night, you can imagine what the dark is like when you're far from home and there's one dingy, smoky kerosene lamp, which for the sake of economy can't be burned long. Imagine lying in a narrow bed with the wind coming in between the rocks and across you, moaning over the inadequate roof. My Aunt Edith lived there, with a family of strangers, during her first year as a schoolteacher. She had finished one year of college when she hired on at the Golden Pond school. She was seventeen. They gave her room and board instead of salary since she wasn't yet of legal age.

Alongside the back porch at 3137 Stadium Drive there is a patio. My father is in it. He died on May 15, 1988, but he was already always there. He brought his cement mixer — the one he made out of doodads and gimcracks and wheels and a motor off something else — and made the first cement to show me how. I watched the swing of the deep-bellied shovel he used, concrete, then gravel, to make what he called *mud* as he tilted a load into my wheelbarrow. He'd make a batch. I'd carry it to the place we'd readied and pour it, and we'd smooth it together. The mud he made was good, though there was no recipe. I guess he knew in his bones and in the arc of the shovel when he had it right. I counted shovelsful to learn the mix. My son and I made the last batches. They're set now, and usable. They still hold. They won't crack before I do. He's mixed in it, and in my arm there's remembrance of the steady swing I learned first making cement with my father.

The first train I knew left Stamford in the morning, came through Aspermont and Jayton and by Gilpin to Spur, then turned around and went back in the afternoon. My father told me about Mr. Fugua, the engineer. I don't know whether my father's memory was accurate, but it's what I have. Mr. Fugua, he said, played a sad song on the train whistle. "I'm here," he'd make the whistle sing, "let me through"; then, "Catch on back there, we're gone." Mr. Fugua's wife left him, my father said, and you'd hear his sad song way down in the shinnery between Swenson and Jayton, "a long cry," my father said, "ending in a sorry laugh. Everybody knew when Mr. Fugua was near the crossing."

Here Brother, hold on. Here, Brother, take this brother's hand. Who left and never returned? Who left, Brother? Here, Brother.

What if I outlive everything I see, or think I see?

What have I lost? I can't recover my own notes, my old notes. What do they mean? What did they mean when I scribbled those fragments: blonde in tight shorts? room above the Neckar? the moment when the lady in the Mercedes looked at me and I looked at her? the medieval ideal of introspective meditation giving way to Faustus's creed of modern activity giving way to the asylum? the poignancy of the lost? What do my own notes mean? Gone. Gone.

They go. They die. Is holocaust a holocaust if you're in it, even if the flame is low, even if the blaze is intermittent?

Some time ago I read in the newspaper that Ken Maynard had died. Lou Gehrig was already long since dead. And Babe Ruth. And Franklin D. Roosevelt. When you get to be fifteen before you realize that anyone else can be president, the rest are just imposters. Now the last of the Big Five was dead. Tom Mix died in 1940 in a car wreck. Buck Jones died in 1942 in the fire at the Coconut Grove. Hoot Gibson died in 1966 of cancer. I don't know what happened to Hopalong Cassidy, but he's gone. And now Ken Maynard was dead at seventy-seven. He made three hundred western movies and sometimes back in the 1930s earned as much as $8,000 a week. But he died in a small house trailer, alone, of physical deterioration and malnutrition. And all those others died. And the list is long, so long.

If your household gods are not regenerative, and they're not, then you're lonesome when they die.

In academic halls, they linger as ghosts. Those others, the old ones, were wise masters who knew everything, mastered their fields, did everything right, and seemed to produce definitive works of scholarship. We learned of them and from them, and even while we were creating new habits of scholarship and new ways of doing things, we heard those ghosts reminding us that we are inadequate, as we always are. They taught us to go about our work in particular ways that we have sometimes abandoned, though only at the cost of anxiety and devaluation. Or we plainly admit defeat, plainly admit that we've gone to Hell, and go searching for new authority to tell us how to behave.

They go. They die. I fail: I cannot, as C. K. Williams writes, lift them "again from the blank caverns of namelessness."

Breece D'J Pancake lived in West Virginia and I don't know where and died in 1975 at age twenty-six by his own hand. Joyce Carol Oates, reviewing his posthumously published stories, says of him:

> The tragic news is that this slender volume is all we will know of Breece D'J Pancake, since he committed suicide in 1979, when he was not quite 27 years old. Precisely why he killed himself at the very start of what promised to be a remarkable career is a mystery, though both James Alan McPherson and John Casey, who knew him as a student in the writing program at the University of Virginia, set forth a number of clues. Breece Pancake (a typesetter once printed his middle initials as D'J, and he adopted the oddity) "didn't know how good he was," Mr. Casey says in his poignant memoir; "he didn't know how much he knew; he didn't know that he was a swan instead of an ugly duckling." But the stories — tense, elegaic, remorseless in their insistence on the past's dominion over the present — argue for a sensibility so finely honed, so vulnerable to the inexorable passage of time, that it is likely death appeared as a solace. As the stories make powerfully clear, Breece Pancake identified so intensely with the coal-mining and farming area of West Virginia in which he was born that he could not have failed to identify with its slow dying as well.

"Come home, come home," the hymn says, "Ye who are weary come home."

Al Young says in *A World Unsuspected*, "I've spent a good chunk of my life trying to prove to my grandfather I could carry a watermelon"; and Dave Smith, in the same book, tells of the death of his grandmother: "Once there's no Queen to call the family together, to cut the pumpkin pie and pour the coffee, the hole is always close."

Some just moved on, and they are gone. Some left, I guess, because they thought they had to: the farm dried up; the wind blew too long, too hard; the place changed; the family came apart.

I have not seen my older daughter for three years. I keep track of the weather where she is. I hope I have it right. On Friday, November 20, 1987, the low was 42, the high 48, and it was cloudy. On Saturday, November 28, there was rain, with a low of 40, a high of 50. On Thursday, January 28, 1988, it was sunny, low 17, high 32.

The days of affliction have taken hold upon me, though most would say that mine are mild. If they are, they're real enough to me, and no acclaim, large or small, will soothe me.

Harold Akey is gone. Uncle Bill is gone. Uncle Dee is gone. Marc Matlock is gone. He died at twenty-one. He was my son's best friend. How many times can you be a pallbearer?

Laddie, a collie, lived for eighteen years and died in Fort Worth. Gulliver, a beagle, lived for thirteen years and died in Fort Worth. "I wanted my dog / to live forever," William Matthews writes,

> and while I was
> working on impossibilities
> I wanted to live forever, too.

I don't know where Grandpa Corder, Robert B. Corder, lived except in Jayton, Texas, where I knew him. He died in 1938 at age fifty-eight. They took him to the hospital in Abilene: the house he lived in was too small to die in. When my father came back from Abilene, he brought my brother and me a new softball. Since the summer of 1938, all evidence notwithstanding, I've thought in a private place that fifty-eight was the age for dying. Last Sunday, September 25, 1988, was my birthday. I made it to fifty-nine, Grandpa.

I don't know where Laura Kidd Corder lived, but she died in Lubbock, Texas. She was a woman of old times; lost, lonesome, and silent for fifteen years after Grandpa died. Grandma made quilts from patterns in her head.

I don't know where Ida Pearl Barton Durham (my grandma, Pearl) lived, but she died near Spur, Texas. She would cook corn on the cob as long as I would eat it, and she made teacakes, and she played Chinese checkers, and I never knew her as she was when I wasn't looking.

Ernest Durham, my grandpa, lived in places I don't know except the farm south of Spur, where he died. You turned off the highway onto two dirt ruts under the trestle, over the cattle guard, and up the slope, the windmill and tank on the left, the house at the top of the rise, the barn beyond it, and beyond that you could see west forever. I do know that ten points a play was a puny score for him at dominoes, and even older men called him Mister. Later, he told my elegant Aunt Edith that he wouldn't go to the nursing home to be fastened up with a bunch of coughing, sneezing, smoking, farting old men.

Nolan Corder lived in places I don't know and in Stonewall County and in Kent County and in Lubbock, and died in Fort Worth on May 15, 1988.

Ruth Corder lived maybe in Denton County and in Stonewall County and in Kent County and in Lubbock, and died in Fort Worth on September 10, 1988.

But David, my son, lives in Cleburne, Texas, with Becky, his wife, and Jennifer, their daughter. Catherine Corder lives in Washington, D.C. Mindy Corder Manson lives in Abilene, Texas, with Bin, her husband, and Andrew, their son.

Beauty and strength and wisdom go before me, go around me, go after me. Why should I grieve?

I grieve for myself. What if all I've known should vanish? The funeral for my mother was on Monday, September 12, 1988. Already on the next day she seemed far away. I grieve for myself. Will it all slip away? What if I outlive all I've seen, or think I've seen?

Beauty and strength and wisdom go before me, go around me, go after me. Why should I grieve?

I grieve for myself. What if all I've known should vanish and leave me alone in the dark?

The ornament that we put on top of the Christmas tree for thirty-four years is broken. My calamities, I guess, are personal and small: nobody starves; nobody is unsheltered; nobody dies — except a little, at my hand. The days of affliction have taken hold upon me, though most would say that mine are mild. If they are, they're real enough to me. They die. They move on. They are gone. Some left, I guess, because they thought they had to: the farm dried up; the wind blew too long, too hard; the place changed; the family came apart.

What if all I think I've known should vanish and leave me alone in the dark?

I can't say grace, can't say "God bless them all," or "may God bless them all," can't make a prayer to serve them all — such effrontery that would be, and why should I be permitted? — can't compose the Mass to tune them all toward Heaven, can't hold a wake, sit shiva for the world: I'm grieving for myself and waiting for the dark.

Beauty and vitality and wisdom and zaniness and hope and quirkiness go before me, go around me, go after me. Why should I grieve? I grieve for myself.

I can't sing praise enough.

I can't commence with "I thank" — such unmitigated gall, my mother would have said, such gall unmitigated in such a verb put after such a subject.

I can't say "bless them," or "God bless them," or "may God bless them," or "I hope that God will bless them." I'm not allowed; or if allowed, not able.

I am not a psalmist or a priest, not a preacher or a prophet; I am neither rabbi nor right.

I can't say it all.

I wait for the dark.

20

I Proposed a New Geography Course, but the Curriculum Committee Turned It Down

I quit gardening in the summer of 1980. In the years I gardened, we had diverse herbs, tomatoes, onions, okra, peppers, radishes, green beans, black-eyed peas, turnips, squash, Jerusalem artichokes—a little dab of some things, a lot of others. That's reason enough to garden. The black-eyed peas alone, when taken with onions and corn bread, made gardening worthwhile.

A garden plot some thirty feet by sixty feet could have, should have, produced considerable amounts of food. I don't know that there is some single reason why I gave that up. I had come to dislike myself in the garden. My own ineptitude kept eroding my hopes for abundance. Even when the crops were decent, they weren't enough to provide good meals through the winter. I expect all of us always hope for plenitude of some kind, whether in goods, pleasures, or freedoms. The garden interfered with this dream of plenitude. The stubbornness of the soil and the chanciness of the weather and my own skill kept teaching me that plenitude might not be within my reach and, worse, it might be the wrong dream.

It was hot. The notes I have record temperatures and rainfall and planting dates. As summer 1980 went on, the notes became briefer and more sporadic, little bleak notations of life at the edge of the Great American Desert.

The garden kept me well acquainted with my own mortality, and a fellow can tolerate only so much of that. At the outset of each season, when the soil had to be turned and mulched and fertilized, I hurt long enough to expect permanent crippling. Thereafter, minor lacerations and contusions and major soreness reminded me that I wasn't the man I used to be, and probably never was.

It was still hot. By June the ground had the aspect of adobe. Before the summer was over we would have almost sixty consecutive days with the temperature over a hundred degrees.

And all along I wasn't diligent enough, and I grew tired of facing my shortcomings in the garden. When I started gardening years ago, I read gardening books and thumbed gardening encyclopedias. I learned reasonably well what one *ought* to do in soil preparation, fertilization, aeration, irrigation, in crop location and plant preparation, but I mostly did it scattershot. I sometimes got sidetracked reading about plants and where they came from and how they got their names, and spent more time with that than I did getting the seeds in the ground by the right phase of the moon.

One morning I went out to the garden early and saw tiny shoots just breaking the ground. Early the next morning I looked again, and the little shoots had already burned. My notes for the previous day showed a temperature of 110 degrees.

I got to thinking about Grandpa Durham. In 1919 he was farming in Denton County. My mother remembered the day vividly. He went into the cotton field to hoe. They saw him stop and bend and look, then move across the field and stop and bend and look. After a while he picked up his hoe and came to the house without looking back.

"Let's pack," he said, "we're going to West Texas." He didn't say more. Later they learned that boll weevils had taken his cotton, and the crop was gone. Nothing was left, not even the future.

When I saw the little shoots burned and twisted, I looked for a while. Then I said, "The hell with it," went in the house, and sat down with a cup of coffee.

Maybe Grandpa Durham would have understood.

Maybe one day I'll find or make another garden.

After great change, in the long later time, will we always mourn for the garden that was, or never was? Perhaps we'll always, as Zulfikar Ghose writes, seek "salvation in a handful of earth." Is every country "an Israel for someone"?

No.

Some don't, I think, look to a place, long for a place, hunt some lost garden; and I wish I knew why some long for places, mourn their loss, while others don't. The explanations I've encountered seem only facile, always unsatisfactory. "I know there are some," Sam Hamill says, "to whom a place is nothing," but some long for their place, he continues:

> This wind lets go
> of everything it touches.
> I long to hold the wind.
> I'd kiss a fish
> and love a stone
> and marry the winter's rain
>
> if I could persuade this battered earth
> to let me make it home.

Some of us do look for places, look toward home, and wonder how often we must be expelled from our places, even if we were never connected. My friend the bird-watcher never lost his connection. He knows the birds and knows where they live. He knows that the nighthawk (one of the North American goatsuckers, kin of the whippoorwill) has bristles around its beak that serve as a funnel for catching flying insects. He knows why the blue jay sometimes lowers its crest, knows where thrashers fly, knows they are sometimes notable singers and mimics. He knows why orchard orioles sometimes settle in wooded parts of town.

I have never known so much, though I've seen birds gone in the sky and usually note their passing. When I was a boy, alone and still on a canyon rim, I tried to count them as they massed and wheeled and rushed away and down and far. Here, now, little that I know of earth is sure. Memory fails with the names I knew, and I never knew most. I've had little to tell my children.

Sometimes I've had time to be out of time, late time, porch time, the moon filigreed by my tree. Once I heard a bird sing, a swift, sweet fluttering hint of blue distance. I leaned against the sound, muttering for the name. Shelley had a name for singers; others had names, designs too, telling what bird on which perch.

But when I heard the bird sing, I didn't know its name. It seems unlikely I'll make a golden bird singing. I stirred in my chair on the porch, and the singer was gone. Since, I've listened: the name of the singer might evoke the song. I wait on the porch.

Some don't look to a place, long for a place, hunt some lost garden, and I wish I knew whether or not they're right. Some do look for places, look toward home, and wonder how many times they must be expelled. Perhaps I'm only afraid, overwhelmed, as Earl Rovit puts it, by a "terror of space," a dread that I might find myself "adrift in a vast uncoordinated fragmentation." Such fear, Rovit suggests, has led many novelists "to reject as arrogant and unworkable that storyteller's Godlike position of omniscience in favor of the fractured focus of the moment and the momentary." Then authority over meaning deserts the writer and enters the jurisdiction of readers, "much as the Protestant Reformation liberated the Bible from the custody of the Church at the eventual cost of depriving the text of its authority." Or perhaps I've only allowed myself to succumb, not to an old longing but to a latter-day foolishness. Southern writing, Marilynne Robinson argues, has been too much preoccupied with "the mystique of past and place." Scots were driven from their land into misery, and blacks were taken from their land to be used as commodities, "with no acknowledgement of their ties to any place or community of family": "This subordination of human beings to sheep on one side of the Atlantic and to cotton on the other is smuggled into our consciousness disguised as an old order, and the noble depopulators and the aristocratic slaveholders as the few, fading survivors of a more human world. History holds few examples of such chutzpah." Perhaps it is only that latter-day foolishness, but I think not. I think it is a melancholy waiting to be recognized, a virulent but not universal melancholy that has come in our century and is the last in the long later time after great change, after death and departure, after the end of a culture, whether we come to know it broadly, as the nations change, or personally, as we faint and waver.

Sometimes, of course, I think it is only that "mystique of past and place" that I have dumbly joined. I have looked for places, have sometimes gone to the places that I thought were the places I was looking for, only to find that they are not refuges and not even dear, though they are inescapable. Some of those places, Tom Asher writes, make

> country too desolate
> to be called geography.

I can't eat viennas and crackers and cheese, drink cheap cold wine, and sit the rest of my life at the head of Putoff Canyon, looking down past the sloping red walls to the blue distance.

I know that much of what I longed to see wasn't real, except in my mind, but then I don't know anything more real. I'm familiar with misbegotten Scots and lost Irishmen, and maybe even understand them. Unthinking. Unthinking to attribute to Walter Scott and to a conditioned mystique what belongs to all, or to many. I don't go to sleep at the Hickman Motel in Aspermont, or to eat the food at Frazier's Restaurant there, because I merely like it or because I am summoned by some mystique. A little mystique doesn't easily continue to pervade and to persuade a life while one knows it is a little mystique.

I long to see places and to know them. I look for the garden that was, or never was, and the places vanish before I can find them. Even if someone wrote to me, I can't get mail from Jayton or Girard or Clairmont or Peacock or Spur or Aspermont or Gilpin. Any letter that reached me from the great beyond, the post office decided, would be postmarked at some central place: Jayton would reach me, if it reached me, and Aspermont, and Gilpin, if it still existed, with a postmark showing Abilene; and even San Angelo, a sizable city, would disappear into Midland. More: for the sake of the scanner down at the post office, whole states with their beautiful names would vanish. Kentucky and Florida and Montana and Oklahoma and Tennessee and Colorado and Texas and Alabama and Arizona and Wyoming would disappear in favor of KY and FL and MT and OK and TN and CO and TX and AL and AZ and WY.

Why would anyone be surprised that young people don't seem to know geography? Afghanistan is on the television and needn't be located. Wyoming has vanished into WY. Geography is not at issue, though the newspapers are sometimes outraged.

Some months ago I proposed a new course to the curriculum committee at the university where I teach. I recommended it as sort of a geography course, though I thought it should bring together literature, history, art, and geography into a place to think about place, what it has meant to us, why a sense of place is strong in some of us but not in others. I'd be glad if I could say that I came to be interested in a geography course because of apparent student needs or because of society's apparent needs. But it did *not* arise out of students' needs or society's needs. It arose out of *my* need, *my* longing to know here, to know there, to know the one in relation to the other.

I have stood more than once in the ruins of Fort Phantom Hill, near Abilene, Texas, and tried to see the place, to know the place. I've read the sane and sober historian's account of the place, and it doesn't sound like the same place described in the memoirs, written much later, by a lady who had lived there as a girl in the 1850s. And neither the historian's fort nor the lady's fort seems much like the fort I created in my imagination out of movies, popular fiction, and wild dreams. And none of these forts looks quite like what I see when I stand in the ruins of Fort Phantom Hill.

It's hard to find places and to know them. T. R. Hummer writes of someone who

> in his dream
> regrets only that he does not know the world so well
> he can be sure every detail of it is true.

Our itinerary: I wish I knew how the places looked to those who came there. I wish I could find the places and see them. How can I see Wolfie's Deli and 845 Michigan Avenue and around the corner and over by 9th Street to the beach in Miami Beach? I wish I knew why we found some places but not others.

At any rate, I proposed what might or might not be a geography course. I thought it would work nicely as a first-year course, mixing a little literature and a little history with a lot of geography, and I thought it would be nice if it were not attached to a single department. I wanted it to be a little quaintly interdisciplinary, and I asked that it be designated a *university* course. I wanted to start with some questions and puzzles and issues: How and why do we acquire so much misinformation about places and their relationships? How do we rhetorically construct a geography for ourselves (the prepositions we use for directions often locate the center of the universe near our various belly buttons)? Why do some people become attached to places while others don't? When and why do we humans begin to think about place? What are our personal geographies?

Then I hoped to go on in the course to learn about places, using the resources available to a citizen—atlases, travel guides, county, state, and federal maps, painting, photographs, poems, novels, histories. I planned to start with the campus as a place and learn its terrain, climate, flora, and fauna, its history; and then, I thought, we'd do the same for the city and the state. No one-term course can *survey* or *cover* much, but it can provide resources and suggestions for continuing study. I was assuming in all of this that we want to know where we are and how, when, and why we got there. Our history offers compelling itineraries. Great and small folk wanderings have happened. Once we learned (as we did in the Renaissance, if not before) that we are in history, then there is a past and there are other places, and they are gone and we ache for them or ignore them at our peril. I wanted to include some guides at least to visual and written works that explore the human sense of place, and to look, too, at film and popular renditions of our concern for place, including nostalgic forms such as coffee-table books, antique stores, and flea markets.

I wanted to remember personal, family, and tribal movements and dislocations—*volkswanderung*, exodus, Renaissance and post-Renaissance explorations, frontier migrations, loss of the frontier, diaspora, holocaust, the great rural-to-urban shift, family dislocations. Sometimes—perhaps often, perhaps always—we spiritually and psychologically reenact in our individual ways the great folk shifts, movements, discoveries, loss. The loss of frontier, for example, and exodus, happen again and again in large and small ways, in public and in intensely private ways. Every generation and every soul, to take another example, has to leap into modernity or to fail to make that leap. This is not something that happened only once, with the Industrial Revolution. Every generation and every soul, for another example, is besieged, surrounded by those who may be hostile. And America, for a last example, and especially its 1988 president, keeps on wanting to be a cowboy clothed in myth — rough riding, straight shooting, at home on the range, and bound for the sunset. We are frontier justice, come to earth to make right and thunder in the dust. We want to die with our boots on. At the same time, we are *not* cowboys, *not* at home on the range, but uprooted, alienated, homeless.

At any rate, I thought our geographies are always discourses waiting to be read, and I wanted at the end of the course to return to some key questions: When did place become important? Why is it important for some but not for others? What happens when we lose our places? Are nostalgia and topophilia going to be persistent human conditions?

Once in a while I think I catch a glimpse of myself and of my people in diverse places with diverse histories, though I never see enough. I have half joked when people inquired why I stayed at my job in Fort Worth all these thirty years. I've told them that there are three reasons: it was an unnecessary cost of spirit and energy to move, I could see the western horizon from my window, and I could get to West Texas quickly if I wanted to. Perhaps I thought — perhaps I still think — that one day I might really learn what the Dust Bowl drought was like. Perhaps lately I began to catch on that what I'd seen was worth seeing, if only I could see it right — that depression, the Dust Bowl times, a rural world just before it changed, a lost world gone in World War II and all that followed, so much and so quickly. Perhaps I came to think that one day I'd really know that country.

But it turned out to be so far. Knowledge is chancy. Evidence disappears. Memory always fails. My interpretation of events is unilateral, but the world isn't. I wanted to find and to know people, events, places. I have studied maps, looking for myself and others, but we aren't there. What I saw, I often saw wrong and then misremembered. Most things I didn't see at all and now can't find.

"Until Henry David Thoreau in the middle of the 19th century," Frederick Turner says, "America had no great literature of place and scarcely even the beginnings of such a tradition." For over two hundred years, he reckons, we didn't learn to make use of the extraordinary lands we called home. Consequently, "before American places had ever been celebrated many of them had been so altered that no one could remember what they had once been like, nor could anyone recall what had once happened in them." Modern readers, he proposes, those who search for some authentic sense of place, become wilderness wanderers, "lost in a thicket of resistance." We might, long ago, have drawn on the oral literatures of native Americans, but we didn't, didn't learn from them to participate emotionally in our living place:

> That surely was one of the functions of the place-rooted myths of old. A part of that emotional identification came through the remembering that the myths inspired, for the places of the myths were the visible reminders of that ancient past that lives in the present, of the enduring and the transitory, of eternity and mortality. So with us and the places and the monuments of our literary landscape. In a culture with so little regard for its lands and for the histories enacted in those lands—all the silent sacrifices sunk like blood into any place—these works in their places remind us to remember. And the end of that remembering is to know again that we do not live in some existential vacuum—and never have.

Mostly, though, we didn't have time, or take time. When we pushed west, Robin Doughty writes, the "thought of untold acreages of fine lands quickened immigrants' pulses. Few people cared whether or for how long the fertility would last. They could always push west." It took a long time for us to guess that places might be more than commodities, might indeed be the "repository or wellspring for nurturing human inspiration and wonder." And when we came to look for and at places and ourselves in them, we had to face what Daniel J. Boorstin describes: "how partial is the remaining evidence of the whole human past, how casual and how accidental is the survival of its relics." What survives, Boorstin observes, is oftener that not (1) what is unread; (2) what is durable and not removed or displaced; (3) what is collected; (4) what is not used but has high intrinsic value; (5) what is academically classifiable and dignified; (6) what is printed about controversies, rather than what is told about dailiness; (7) what is self-serving, as in diaries and letters; (8) what is victorious; (9) what cannot be experienced personally; and (10) what people come to know, but not the ignorance they practiced.

And so how do we find earth? I read a new item about drawing-board schemes for reaching the far sides of space. One plan for overcoming the prohibitive time it will take even at fantastic speeds to reach other galaxies calls for a huge globe to be equipped on various levels with power stations, water supply, smaller rocket ships, repair, maintenance, and construction workshops, artificially provided farmland and livestock areas, schools, hospital facilities, and entertainment. Into this would go five hundred couples. Their distant progeny would be our pioneers in the dark frontiers.

We have not commanded morning or measured all of earth, but we wish to outrace time to its most curious ends, where space, for all I know, bends back next door. One day we'll buzz a warning, count, and throw new globes in fire from the earth, grown a metaphor for sun, from out whose burning, they say, earth long since crackled and cooled. Maybe then they'll wonder, maybe now we wonder, who sits at what console to monitor our seeing, and who is her God, his? Maybe they'll find themselves watched, and sing, turn toward some console, repent, bow, and pray. Maybe they'll find themselves, or we ourselves, merely specimens. Maybe they'll turn metaphor again, and from that new earth, humming busily in the great dark, cast out another world and never know ourselves hurled aloft those years ago. We have not commanded morning, have not found the dayspring's place. We have lost the earth of plowing, do not hear the killdee's sound, but wonder, ourselves and them, Who watches? Who is her God or his? If throwing earths from out of earth we lay new time in space, then which earth was Adam's, which place is ours?

Some don't look to a place, long for a place, hunt some lost garden, and I wish I knew whether or not they're right. Some do look for places, look toward home, and wonder how many times they must be expelled. After great change, in the long later time, will we always mourn for the garden that was, or never was? The places change or vanish, or I can't find them, or I find them and can't see them. I have studied maps, looking for myself, for others, for places, but we aren't there. What I saw, I often saw wrong and then misremembered. Most things I didn't see at all and now can't find.

Maps

SEPARATE

1. A book, *County Maps of Texas*, one county per each ten-by-fourteen-inch page. They gave it to me for Christmas.

2. Six enlarged maps, approximately eighteen by twenty-six inches, of Stonewall, Kent, Dickens, King, Haskell, and Garza counties.

IN THE BOX

1. A city map of Washington from the May 1988 trip. On the back, addresses are scribbled — two restaurants and two pipe shops. With the map are a Metro System Pocket Guide, a magazine called *Where Washington*, and a restaurant guide, with 399 listed.

2. A city map and restaurant guide for New Orleans.

3. A city map of Philadelphia.

4. Maps and notes from Chicago and Evanston, city maps for each, and a magazine, *North Shore*. The notes are on napkins and on a notepad from the North Shore Hilton in Skokie. I scribbled how I walked south on Chicago Avenue in Evanston to the newsstand, where I turned west on Washington, then south again on Custer to the apartment where Cathy lived in 1977 and 1978. Then I went back into the center of Evanston, by Fritz That's It, and over to the Holiday Inn, where we waited for her that time. I guess I was looking for it to be the same, wanting the world to be the same, wanting the world to be the same and it never was.

5. The maps Cathy gave me for Christmas — Caney Creek Wil-

derness, Caddo–Lyndon B. Johnson Grasslands, Davy Crockett National Forest. I loaned the others to friends for their fishing expeditions.

6. A group standing sideways in the box, alongside the others — maps of Texas, New Mexico, Fort Worth, Colorado, Texas state parks, the Texas Independence Trail, Oklahoma, and Memphis, with folders on Mission Conception, San Jose Mission, Mission San Juan, Mission Espada, and LaGrange.

7. A package from AAA on the other Washington trip, with a U.S. map, guidebooks on Kentucky, Tennessee, Delaware, the District of Columbia, Maryland, Virginia, and West Virginia, with an emergency road service directory, a folder on Gatlinburg, and a note giving directions to Cathy's apartment.

8. Remains of a trip to the Davis Mountains, with folders on the Davis Mountains, Fort Davis, Indian Lodge, and Carlsbad Caverns.

9. Another group on that Washington trip, with a map of the Museum of Natural History, folders for Monticello, the Washington Cathedral, and the National Gallery of Art, and copies of *Washington Post Weekend*, *The Hill Rag*, and *The Georgetowner*.

10. A copy of the *Evanston Review* for October 27, 1977.

If you go home to the past — or try — to find yourself in the present and to guess out a future, and the past is gone, then what? And where are you? If you study maps to find where you were or are, and you aren't there, then what? I have followed maps to Stonewall County, but the house where I was born is gone. Most of the houses where I have lived are gone, and I'm not in those that remain.

But I've made my way through maps, sometimes with great pleasure, sometimes thinking secretly that I've made a pilgrimage. In July 1987 I privately thought I made my own little epic through maps. When you're not heroic, you take your bravery where you find it. It began on July 4. Used to, we'd take the day off, go slow, putter a little, lazy around, but I'd get a good fire going early — mesquite, you know, soaked to give good smoke — and set a brisket cooking at the end away from the fire, nice and easy and slow in the smoke. Slow's the way for brisket. Sometimes, when the fire was strong and steady, I'd also cook maybe some hot links or chicken or a stick of salami. She'd fix up other stuff—potato salad, maybe beans. By and by it would all be done, with maybe a mixer full of ice cream. Whoever came by could eat. If no one came, we'd eat it all ourselves, sooner or later. This wasn't habitual, but it happened often enough to be clear and dear.

But what is there of *used to* that anyone can count on? On July 4, 1987, from a little before 6:00 A.M., I found myself on the road for Memphis and beyond.

I had driven close to 600 miles in a day before, but never alone. I don't believe I had even driven alone more than about 225 miles, from Fort Worth to San Angelo. This time I was alone, and I would drive much farther. On July 4 I drove 522 miles; on July 5 I drove 666 miles; on July 6 I drove 295 miles—total so far, 1,483 miles.

The first day took me through Dallas, by Rockwall, to Greenville, where I stopped for breakfast at 7:15, then on by Mount Vernon and Mount Pleasant and Hooks, and through Texarkana into Arkansas, and by Hope, Prescott, and Arkadelphia, and through Little Rock, and on to a roadside park beyond Hazen, where I stopped for lunch out of the picnic basket and the ice chest, and on across the Mississippi, and to a Holiday Inn at the east edge of Memphis—522 miles.

Since I didn't sleep well, I left Memphis early and stopped in Jackson, Tennessee, for breakfast. After 622 miles I passed the exit for Barren Hollow Road. At 667 miles I passed the exit for Bucksnort. At 726 miles I crossed the Cumberland River in Nashville, and at 738 miles I passed the exit for Long Hollow Pike. At 763 miles I crossed into Kentucky. At a decimal or two over 1,000 miles I crossed the Ohio River into Ohio, and at 1,188 miles, after I got lost in Zanesville, I stopped there for the night at another Holiday Inn—for the day, 666 miles, for the trip so far, 1,188 miles, a new record, and more to come.

On July 6, at 1,257 miles, I crossed the Ohio River at Wheeling into West Virginia, and at 1,269 miles I crossed into Pennsylvania. At 1,312 miles I crossed the Monongahela River. At 1,483 miles

I arrived at University Park, Pennsylvania, at the Sheraton Penn State, 295 miles for the day, 1,483 miles for the trip. More was to come, but I'd be there for a conference for four days, had already made my little pilgrimage, reached about as much bravery as I'll get, seen sweet rivers and hazy hills, and had read the beautiful names on the road signs and the maps. The solitary portion of the trip ended at about 2,000 miles at Logan Airport in Boston, where I met her plane. The hills and rivers and roadside names receded in the rearview mirror, but she remained.

Is our preoccupation with sexual pleasure both a preoccupation with sexual pleasure and a version of the search for the dear place we can surely know? I don't know. But I studied her topography, and she mine, that night and the next and the next; hills, mounds, crevices, caverns, textures, tastes, right-side up, upside down, front side, back side, and I was there.

Sometimes I go hunting for places to see if I'm there, and I'm not; can't see either places or self. Maybe I don't get aimed to see well.

If you go home to the past to find the present and the future, and the past is gone, then what? If you hunt for places to see if you're there, and you're not, and you can't see either places or self, then what?

Maps

SEPARATE

1. The Rand McNally Road Atlas of the United States, Canada, and Mexico. The cover has come off.

IN THE STACK ON MY DESK

1. A street map of St. Louis.
2. "Dining in Columbia," with a street map.
3. Another map and guide to Chicago.
4. The rest of the 1987 summer trip, including a map of Ocean Creek, North Carolina, maps of the southeastern states, of the White Mountains, of Maine, New Hampshire, Vermont, Connecticut, Massachusetts, Rhode Island, Kentucky, Tennessee, North Carolina, South Carolina, Alabama, Georgia, Boston and

vicinity, guidebooks for the same states, folders on the Franconia Notch, the Coach and Eagle Trail in Concord, and the New Hampshire seacoast.

5. A package of materials from Johnson City and Jonesborough, Tennessee, and the Blue Ridge Parkway.

The Riga that Ilse Rothrock knew just before World War II is gone, and I will never see it or Bucharest or Budapest, though a new Riga, where Latvian is once again spoken, is being built.

I sometimes miss Mannheim and Germany, though I didn't see them even when I was there. We left on a troopship on July 4, 1951 (such pilgrimages, that begin on July 4); we came back in late November 1952. I was in the Fifty-seventh Medium Tank Battalion, part of the Second Armored Division. We were stationed at Coleman Barracks, just outside Mannheim.

Many blocks of the city were still rubble then, and the bridges over the Neckar and the Rhine were new and only serviceable. I don't know how often Mannheim was bombed. The bombing began on December 16, 1940, when 134 planes of the Royal Air Force Bomber Command raided the city. From that time until March 1945, when Mannheim fell, there were other raids, though probably not as many as my imagination told me. Some 730 bombers attacked Mannheim and Ludwigshafen on August 14, 1944, and by December 1944 the area was deemed one of eight key points for bomber concentration. Between December 26 and December 31, 1944, 5,516 heavy bombers dropped 14,177 tons of explosives on a quadrangle including Mannheim. On February 1, 1945, about 700 heavy bombers attacked the city. General Omar Bradley gives an account of the setting for the end: "Midway between its headwaters in the Alps and its North Sea Delta, the Rhine turns at Mainz before plunging into the gorge that speeds it downstream to Bonn. Between Mannheim and Mainz the river flows through the grassy plains of Hesse with its broad level banks and easy path to the industrial environs of heavily bombed Frankfurt. It was toward these plains that Patton had aimed his armored spearheads." By March 23, the Third Army was across the Rhine, and before the end of the month, Mannheim had fallen.

I knew none of that in 1951. The rooms, the houses, were alien, oblivious to me, and I to them. The ruins were abstract and dehumanized. I don't know where I was when the tank scraped the corner of that house. I remember a church where Mozart played, now ruined. I remember stairs that went up to nothing. Mostly I remember doorways, especially near die Wasserturm, with no walls, strong doors, beautiful doors. I remember Het Witte Paard in Rotterdam. I remember walking along the Neckar. I remember Remy's and the Rodensteiner. I remember the castle above Heidelberg. I remember walking and walking and walking. I remember stairs that went up to nothing. Mostly I remember doorways with no walls. I remember the rooms of strangers, with pictures of Bismarck and of young soldiers from the 1914–18 war and young soldiers from the 1939–45 war. Some of them looked very like my brother. Some of them looked very like me. But I was not there. I, too, was abstracted, dehumanized, unaware. Knowledge fails.

There is no wasteland: there is only land we have not come to know. Or if we thought we knew, we have lost it, cannot find it. I remember a dust storm. I watched it from my office window that let in the west-northwest, where God lives on top of the Double Mountains. I couldn't see the Double Mountains. They are too far—five hours away, supposing I could get away. I couldn't see God. He (or She, as the case may be) was, is, too far, maybe ten billion miles, or on the Double Mountains, or all the way next door. She (or He, as the case may be) might have been just across the way. I couldn't see just across the way from my window that gave upon God and the west-northwest. I could see the nearest buildings and the first row of live oaks. Beyond that, dust. The horizon was gone, and beyond the first trees the world was all one color, one shape, one style. Outside, the old thrill was there for a moment, as when God rides down out of the west-northwest on a hard blue norther, or rides the whirlwind, rides the dust gale down the Caprock. Outside, I saw one small reach farther, saw the stadium outlined brown against the dust, saw a second row of trees, scarcely sketched. I heaved and breathed gladly and felt God for a moment in the wind and plenty of life, but could not see house, home, horizon, high, far, or God.

I long to see the places, the places I knew, the places I never knew, but they vanish even while I look. How many times must we be expelled? Some are never expelled, if T. R. Hummer is correct in his poem "The Rural Carrier Discovers That Love Is Everywhere":

A registered letter for the Jensens. I walk down their drive
Through the gate of their thick-hedged yard, and by God
   there they are,
On a blanket in the grass, asleep, buck-naked, honeymooners,
Not married a month. I smile, turn to leave,
But can't help looking back. Lord, they're a pretty sight,
Both of them, tangled up in each other, easy in their skin —
It's their own front yard, after all, perfectly closed in
By private hedge and country. Maybe they were here all night.

I want to believe they'd do that, not thinking of me
Or anyone but themselves, alone in the world
Of the yard with its clipped grass and fresh-picked fruit trees.
Whatever this letter says can wait. To hell with the mail.
I slip through the gate, silent as I came, and leave them
Alone. There's no one they need to hear from.

But some are expelled — and leave — every day. In his poem "The Gardener" Stephen Dobyns tells how God retired to a little brick cottage "after the first astronauts reached heaven":

                  He was not
unduly surprised. He had seen it coming
since Luther. Besides, what with the imminence
of nuclear war, his job was nearly over.

God remembers that "his particular talent was as a gardener," and recalls

How pleasant Eden had been in those early days
with its neat rows of cabbages and beets,
flowering quince, a hundred varieties of rose.

Remembering that when he had thought "to make something /
really big," he'd meant it to be "a kind of scarecrow to stand in
the middle / of the garden and frighten off predators":

> What
> voice had he listened to that convinced him
> to give the creature his own face? No voice
> but his own.

Then he muses that he had not expelled the creature, not at all:

> When had he realized his mistake? Perhaps
> when he smiled down at the first and it
> didn't smile back; when he reached down to help
> it to its feet and it shrugged his hand aside.
> Standing up, it hadn't walked on the paths marked
> with white stones but on the flowers themselves.
> It's lonely, God had said. So he made it a mate,
> then watched them feed on each other's bodies,
> bicker and fight and trample through his garden,
> dissatisfied with everything and wanting to escape.
> Naturally, he hadn't objected. Kicked out,
> kicked out, who had spread such lies? Shaking
> and banging the bars of the great gate, they had
> begged him for the chance to make it on their own.

Places I Can't Find or See,
Places I Can't Tell About

1. An article in the July–August issue of the *Texas Humanist*
titled "Water Politics: Making Plans before the Well Runs Dry"
tells of diverse plans to make the dry parts green. I don't think I'll
see it, but I'm not sure: back in the 1930s the citizens of Jayton
planted over five hundred trees, and the little town is greener by
far than I remember.

2. An article from the Sunday *New York Times* travel section,
titled "Around America by Rail," subhead "8000 Miles, 5 Amtrak
Trains, 1 Case of Champagne—All in 2 Weeks" (May 13, 1984),
tells about riding the Crescent from New York to New Orleans,

the Sunset Limited from New Orleans to Los Angeles, the Coast Starlight from Los Angeles to Seattle, the Empire Builder from Seattle to Chicago, the Lake Shore Limited from Chicago to New York. I guess I won't see all that.

3. Another article from the *Times* (November 11, 1979) is titled "You Can Still Ride the Rails for Scenery and for Fun." I probably won't.

4. A story in the November 16, 1975, *Fort Worth Star Telegram* is headed "Scientist Believes Drought Overdue for Great Plains." I've probably seen that, but can't tell it right.

5. The *Star Telegram* for July 24, 1983, has two stories, "West Texas Weather: A Forecast by Contrast," and "If the Weather Is Normal, It Can't Be West Texas." I've seen most of the weather but can't trust my memory.

6. Another *Star Telegram* story, for June 23, 1974, says "Famine Possibility Predicted." Maybe it's already come for some.

7. C. C. Rister's "The Border Post of Phantom Hill," in the *West Texas Historical Association Year Book* for October 1938, gives a good short history of "one of the loneliest stations along the entire Texas frontier." I've seen the chimneys and foundations—all that remains—but can't get situated with the sun right to see it as all those others did, the troops from 1851 to 1854, memoirists and historians since.

8. I've driven west on Interstate 20 and passed by Putnam, population 203 in 1966, when Larry King wrote about it in "Requiem for a West Texas Town" (*Harper's*, January 1966), but I surely can't see what he saw—home. "How could a place be allowed to die?" he asked. "But the anger passed, for I knew I would not find the answer—not this side of whatever Heaven there is that has rewarded all Putnamites who lived by the code. And even then the answer would probably lie on the farther slope of the last holy hill, guarded by a mean old dog."

9. I have a quick drawing of their gravestones, four low pink marble stones. One, centered on one side, says only CORDER. Two are at either side of the plot. One says ROBERT B. CORDER, JUNE 18, 1877–JULY 23, 1938. The other says LAURA CORDER, SEPT. 1, 1881–APR. 19, 1953. The fourth, centered opposite the CORDER stone,

says RESTING TOGETHER. I knew them, and didn't. I wish I could have seen from their eyes. The graves are on the western edge of the Jayton cemetery. It's close to being the loneliest place I know.

10. The *New York Times Book Review* for August 18, 1985, carries a review of Carole Krinsky's *Synagogues of Europe*. I haven't seen them. None of us will see those destroyed in the 1930s and 1940s.

11. An article from *Texas Highways* (March 1987) tells about the "Flower of the Sun," helianthus, most frequently *Helianthus annuus*. I have looked at them all my life, but I never learned them well enough to know their yield — for Anglos: soups, snacks, oils, parched seeds ground into flour or dripped for near-coffee; for Indians: a tea against malaria, boiled roots against poison ivy, crushed roots against snakebite, yellow dye from the flower, black and purple dye from the seeds, thread from the fibrous stalk.

12. Two articles in the *Star Telegram* (October 6, October 7, 1984) under the general title, "West Texas Travel Guide." The section on the Panhandle and High Plains features Amarillo, Canyon, Palo Duro Canyon State Park, the Alibates Monument, Caprock Canyon, Lubbock, and more. The section on the central trails features Abilene, Buffalo Gap, San Angelo, Del Rio, Langtry, Midland, Big Springs, Monahans, Fort Stockton, Pecos, the Guadalupe Mountains, El Paso, Fort Davis, and more. I've seen most, but never well enough.

13. The *New York Times Book Review*, October 23, 1977, reviewed Uwe George's *In the Deserts of the Earth*, and I went quickly to own the book. The desert, he says, will win, is already winning. I think I've seen that, but I can't tell it.

14. An article in the *Texas Humanist* for May–June 1983, "The FW & DC Railroad," chronicles the building of railroads west and north from Fort Worth on out through the Panhandle. One branch line, sometimes known as the Wichita Valley line, part of it known as the Stamford and Northwestern line, came down from Wichita Falls, turned at Stamford one way toward Abilene, the other way toward Aspermont, Jayton, and Spur. My father worked those lines in the 1920s, first running a wood burner, then as a section foreman. My mother followed him in their car, pulling a little house trailer they had built. I haven't found the line

my father told me about, the CRI and GOP, better known as the "Cry and Go Pee Line," and I haven't learned to see it, haven't learned to see their territory, or mine.

15. The travel section of the Sunday *New York Times*, September 26, 1976, tells "What's Doing along the Shenandoah," from Stanton to Harper's Ferry. I wish I knew.

16. A *Star Telegram* article on March 25, 1985, says "Farmers Snapping under Stress," and reports suicides and other grim extremes "among thousands of farmers nationwide facing bankruptcy or foreclosure." How could I see what they have seen when they look out across the fields?

17. The *Star Telegram* reports on January 22, 1981, that "Aspermont Pastor Bans Club for Flock." Seems that the folks down at Frazier's Café, not far off the square, have applied for a liquor license and will open a private club there. I've been there more than once since, have surely enjoyed the drinks. Mr. Frazier's father-in-law was minister of the Methodist church. I wonder how things were at Sunday dinner.

18. Mason Williams sang back in 1970:

> I've got to ask the question, cause the
> answer's overdue:
> Why can't we all ride out together, and be
> cowboy buckaroos?

I pretty seriously wanted to be Hopalong Cassidy—never Gene Autry or Roy Rogers—until I was about ten, but I never thought about it much afterward.

19. In the movie, *Little Big Man*, Old Lodge Skins, as played by Chief Dan George, says, "There is an endless supply of white men, but there always has been a limited number of human beings. We won today. We won't win tomorrow." Maybe no one will. In the movie *Monte Walsh*, Jack Palance says to Lee Marvin, "Nobody gets to be a cowboy forever." I almost see.

20. A *Star Telegram* article on March 26, 1972, bears the headline "Let Some Small Towns Die, Presidential Panel Urges." I guess it was wise of the panel to ratify the inevitable. Some towns die. More will. How will we ever see them all, get testimony?

21. The city map of Galveston shows me all the streets I walked in the spring of 1983, but doesn't show me what I saw.

22. I've been to Soldier Mound, between Spur and Dickens, more than once, but I only just now learned, from Frank Tolbert's column in the August 31, 1965, *Dallas Morning News* (it's been in my files for twenty-three years) that "atop this high sandstone headland there is a bullet-pocked historical marker, placed there in 1936. The granite marker has been knocked down, and vandals have pried loose the copper medallion." I look, and don't see.

23. I have a small spiral notebook with notes I made in August 1964 during a trip to Jayton and Spur with my family. It was the first time I'd ever gone back with time to look since 1939. For twenty-five years I had thought that the statue in front of the Stonewall County Courthouse in Aspermont was of a Confederate soldier. It was a statue of Justice. Uncle Alec Kidd's farm and Uncle John Kidd's farm were north of the highway from Aspermont to Jayton, west of the Salt Fork. Uncle Jack Kidd's farm was south of the highway. They were my father's uncles. Aunt Edith remembered that as a young teenager in the early 1920s she couldn't mention the Ku Klux Klan to her friends; feelings were too strong. In that territory the Klan was as much or more concerned with the proper behavior of poor whites as with black people — there were more of the one than the other to occupy the Klan's piety. In 1964 the trestle was still there below Grandpa's farmhouse, and the game was still okay: I ran down one side, and the momentum carried me almost to the top on the other side. On Saturday night we played dominoes with Grandpa. He said his family came from around Durham, North Carolina, then went to northern Georgia, then to middle Tennessee, then to around Denton in north Texas. He told of going to a family reunion in Denton one time. He found that his Uncle Rufe was listed in family papers as a deserter, but he made them change that. He said his Uncle Rufe fought for three days at Gettysburg, and then, his arm shot up, rode his mule home to Georgia, so beat up and skinny by the time he got there that his mother didn't recognize him. When he got well, he rejoined the army, this time in Texas.

Grandpa said he heard about the war from his Uncle Rufe; they worked side by side in the fields, he said.

After great change, in the long later time, will we always mourn for the garden that was, or never was? Some don't look to a place, hunt some lost garden, and I wish I knew whether or not they're right. I have studied maps, looking for myself, for others, but we aren't there. What I saw, I often saw wrong and then misremembered. Most things I didn't see at all and now can't find, or I find them and can't see them. What is there of *used to* that anyone can count on? If you go home to the past to find yourself, and you're not there, then what? And where are you? I long to hold the wind.

24. In 1971 they hired a rainmaker in Aspermont. He came in February and promised to make it rain five inches in thirty days for a fee of $10,000. By March 11, the last report I had, an inch had fallen. He took credit for that inch. I remember watching my folks when they watched the sky, but I didn't see what they were looking for.

25. A page full of related stories appear in the *Star Telegram* on Sunday, October 31, 1954, under the general heading, "Oil Developers Help Farm, Ranch Communities Keep Good Income." Separate stories carry these headlines: "Irrigation Gets Start in Dickens"; "New Courthouse and Bank in Wind for Kent County"; "Building in Stonewall to Cost Nearly Million"; "Spur is Hospital, Bank and Recreation Center." Among the pictures was a photograph of the Jayton school, the old red-brick building that I remember from the 1930s. It's not there anymore. I can't see it, and of course I can't see the new building, though I've been inside. An article in the *Abilene Reporter-News* for April 17, 1988, says that "thanks to its wealth, the Jayton-Girard Independent School District is a leader among Texas schools." Property taxes raise less than 4 percent of the district's revenues, and the state provides only about $50,000. The rest comes from oil properties, income enough to support an expenditure of $8,845 per pupil in 1986–87.

26. The September 1986 issue of *Texas Highways* has an article

titled "High Country Oasis," about the Davis Mountains State Park. I've been there. I've looked closely. A two-page photograph shows the Limpia valley. The foreground is still in blue shadows from the mountain where the photographer is standing, but the sun shines directly on Indian Lodge and the mountains behind it. We walked those mountains once, but will not again.

Some time back, Craig Clifford reported that "a lot of people aren't from anywhere." That's true, and maybe not. Most of us, even those not pulled toward some particular territory, long for the place that was, or the place that we thought was, or the place that will be.

27. Mr. C. W. Post intended to find or make a Utopia out on the Caprock and just below, on that beautiful red earth. He helped build the town that's named for him, but he went back to making cereal after deep wells failed to find sufficient water in the breaks below the Caprock and after his "rain battles" of 1910 and 1911 failed, too. Maybe the most spectacular was on April 6, 1911. From fifteen stations along about two miles of the rim of the Caprock, starting at 2:07 P.M. and ending at 5:48 P.M., 1,500 three-pound rounds of dynamite were exploded. It rained that time, but it mostly didn't after his battles. He had interesting ideas: he wanted to convert cotton to cloth on the ground where it was raised, and beets to sugar. Post is about forty-five straight miles from Jayton. Post didn't turn out to be Utopia for him, or Jayton for me, though it might have if I'd known how to look.

28. "We'll find the place," the Mormons sang,

> which God for us prepared,
> Far away in the West,
> Where none shall come to hurt or make afraid;
> There the saints will be blessed.

I guess not.

29. In his book *Rivers of Empire*, Donald Worster suggests that hydraulic engineers have "had more to do with making the modern West than all the fur trappers and cowboys and sheepherders

there ever were." It's probably not what Hopalong Cassidy expected, but Hoppy left. That old dream of the West as a refuge of freedom has gone or changed; the original intention of the Homestead Act, to sustain an agrarian republic of small farms, has not been fulfilled. Hoppy left.

30. Milan Kundera remarked in an interview once, "If someone had told me as a boy: one day you will see your nation vanish from the world, I would have considered it nonsense, something I couldn't possibly imagine."

31. In his essay "Home: An American Obsession," in *Saturday Review* for November 26, 1977, Reynolds Price writes:

> It was only with the first generation *born here* that what had seemed a clean impulse to freedom began to seem a doom instead, a curse in the seed. The children grew on the labor involved in clearing land or spinning thread to feed family mouths; then once grown, they tore loose and lost themselves in the unimaginable distances provided by America — The Cumberland Gaps, the plains and forests so patiently eager to swallow and hide. Think of all the sons and daughters — labored over, nurtured for years in the natural hope of eventual return (a tended old age) — who one day said plain farewells and rode off westward, out of sight and voice forever: no phones, no regular mail, *disappearance*. Any country's history may be seen with some justice as a series of dramatic genres — tragedy, farce, melodrama, vaudeville turn. A large part of eighteenth and nineteenth-century American history was a vanishing act; a large part still is.

32. A *Star Telegram* column by Brian Dickinson on November 28, 1987, is headed, "Get Kids Back to the Map to Learn Our Place in the World." Maps are good, but they won't tell. The boundaries on maps are mostly drawn by someone else, and it's usually someone else who seems to know the territory. The small geography that each of us is the center of does not always appear on maps drawn by others.

33. I can't see the house at 3137 Stadium Drive. What if my

memory of it turns out to be as unreliable as my memory of other places?

I long to see places and to know them. They are destroyed, or they vanish as I move away. How many times must we be expelled? I look toward home, ready to be sad. Such migrations we've made. How far we've come. Most gardens are far away.

21

The Ache for Home

For a long time, I guess, I assumed that only some people—
say those of certain generations, or those in certain locations, or
those in circumstances of dislocation—experienced any sense of
nostalgia. Sometimes I thought I knew why; sometimes I didn't.
Surely we can understand when I. B. Singer says that "literature
has neglected the terrible trauma of those who are forced to leave
their land, abandon their language and begin a new life somewhere else"; and mostly we'll nod with Reynolds Price when he
speaks of "the idea of home as icon and amulet, gross sentimen-
tality and bedrock truth simultaneously." If we stay at home, we
must watch it change and die; if we escape home, then "time finds
us anywhere, the ultimate police." Some always remember, I expect, that we are fugitives and vagabonds in the earth, that we
are dust:

> As for man, his days are as grass: as a flower of the field, so he
> flourisheth.
>
> For the wind passeth over it, and it is gone; and the place
> thereof shall know it no more.

But now I believe otherwise. Nostalgia is not singular or particular, not unique to those who live in certain generations or
in certain locations or among particular dislocations. It is not an
aberration, and not a social disease. It is what we live once we fall
into history.

After great change, or any change that seems great, in the *later*
time, which may be long but sometimes rushes, we all experience
nostalgia, though it takes many forms; sometimes surfaces, sometimes submerges, sometimes masks itself. We are always nostalgic.
Some express nostalgia directly and readily, though my expres-

sion will be different from yours. Some are nostalgic unawares, expressing only masked versions.

And there is more: nostalgia is always accompanied by a conflict of tongues, by the failure of memory, and by the threat of personal invisibility. And there is more: we always come into this world educated in the wrong curriculum. None is the cause of the others or the result of the others. They accompany each other, always in the presence of each other. If there is a cause, it is change itself, and there is always great change: the world always comes unfixed, and we're always having to try to fix it.

Nostalgia may be quiescent or insistent, may occur in exalted moments or in depressed moments or in trivial moments or in an undifferentiated tangle: Thomas Gray aches for, imagines, but cannot find the rustic poet–stonecutter in his "Elegy," and "Golden Days" pulls at us even if we're not old and haven't been to the inn in Heidelberg, and we wonder who we were before we were who we are and what were we like in the old days, and we berate ourselves for such small sadness against the loss of Diaspora and Holocaust, and we think that never seeing the farmhouse again is hurtful, too, and we see presidential candidates campaigning for the world of John Wayne and Norman Rockwell, and we remember the family members in *A Fiddler on the Roof* who may never see each other again, or we feel a twist of wind down out of the northwest late on a fall afternoon, and on, and on. Old time calls, and not just sentimentally: Simone Weil says, in *The Need for Roots*, that "loss of the past, whether it be collectively or individually, is the supreme human tragedy." People depart or die. Places change. We can never catch events in our memory just as they were.

The people are lonely when the gods that inhabited the old places disappear or die, even if the gods weren't all that much in the first place. The speaker in George Garrett's "Goodbye Old Paint, I'm Leaving Cheyenne," remembering Buck Jones and Tom Mix, watches a television western with his children; he shrinks and becomes "a boy with a sweaty nickel in his palm," and sees that everything has changed:

Children, this plot is new to me.
I watch the Hero take the wrong road
at the Fork and gallop away, grim-faced,
worn out from the exercise of choice.
I see the Badmen safely reach the Gulch,
then fight among themselves and die,
proving good luck is worse than any wound.
My children stare and couldn't care
less about my fit of raw nostalgia
or all the shabby ghosts I loved and lost.

Owen Wister already knew that the world he wrote about had vanished, but Ted Gray holds on in *The Last Campfire*: "Every cowboy has hope that, somewhere up there on the high ranges above, the grass will be forever green, the water plentiful, the cattle fat, and his faithful horse will never tire." Still, that's another world he hopes for—the old one is gone. In 1932 Douglas Southall Freeman ended his essay, "The Last Parade"—written for Civil War veterans returning for a reunion at Richmond—with this: "The armies of the South will march our streets no more. It is the rear guard, engaged with death, that passes now. Who that remembers other days can face that truth and still withhold his tears? The dreams of youth have faded in the twilight of the years. The deeds that shook a continent belong to history. Farewell; sound taps! And then a generation new must face its battles in its turn, forever heartened by that heritage." But the heritage of one age, we learn, sometimes slowly, sometimes all too suddenly, doesn't always strengthen us in another.

Who knows what losses come? Even the hated dead can finally be mourned, and those once known as enemies can be allowed to grieve. Wendelgard von Staden, in *Darkness over the Valley*, re-members Harvest Day, a Sunday in October just before World War II broke out in Europe, remembers the songs they sang: "Many who sang these songs with us then, later lost their lives. Young Schank was killed at the very beginning of the war. Gunther Guller and the Linkenheils boys never returned, nor did Wilhelm

Gutjahr. Reinhold Kuhner was listed as missing on the eastern front. I cannot remember whether the church bells were rung at the end of our war. I don't believe they were. But as we sang about the black hood of Death and mothers visiting their sons' graves, we had no idea of what lay ahead of us." Horst Kruger, in *A Crack in the Wall*, tells of returning after long years to his home in Berlin, of thinking about his father and mother and sister, all dead:

> I carry within myself the weight of three people who were once alive. I barely knew them, but they live in me now and will die only with me. That's what is meant by family, Eich-kamp family—it's so long ago. In me it all comes together, and if I were a decent person, I would pack up and move to Berlin, I would visit their graves regularly.
>
> The last survivor is always something like a cemetery cus-todian.

Later, he adds: "All are almost forgotten. Time, they say, heals all wounds. But is that really true? Isn't it rather that time inflicts new wounds, wounds that never heal?"

"Nothing, not even the land," Louise Erdrich writes, "can be counted on to stay the same." For Hawthorne, Cather, Faulkner, and others, "it is therefore as if, in the very act of naming and describing what they love, they lost it." We can remember, but not recover, and our remembering is mostly inaccurate, though what's in there is real enough and more than dear, even if it's not exactly on the map. We all have a place, Stephen Dobyns pro-poses, "where we feel safest, even if it is only / the idea of a place," perhaps something simple "like the memory of a back porch / where we laughed a lot." In "Trip to Bountiful" Michael Blumen-thal writes, "yes, it is good not to be alone / at times like these," when his companion sobs and says "It's / so sad, this movie,"

> and you agree, yes,
> it *is* very sad, this movie, and this life
> in which so much we imagine as inalterable
> will be taken from us, in which
> there are so many towns where someone

will die, this very day, alone and unclaimed
by any of their loved ones (who have all left
to marry in another country or find their fortunes
in some greed-stricken Houston)
which is why it is good to be here,
even just tonight, in this dimly lit theater,
with a good woman and the scent of popcorn
and a wide bed you can climb into again together,
as if it were the town you originally came from
and you could always go back to it,
as if no one could even die in the dark alone,
not even you.

Perhaps. All my samples piled up, even heap on heap, wouldn't *prove* that we're all always in nostalgia, and they'd not be another's samples anyway. I remember when we backed out of the driveway that time in Spur. My mother and my father and Grandpa Durham stood side by side in the yard, waving to us as we went, and I thought that we might not see each other again, and now we won't. I have wanted to know the names of people and places and things so that I could hold them in my mind, have wanted to get situated just so with the sun so that I might see, just so, the scenes I remember and hold moments forever. Photographs don't work; I have taken pictures, only to discover later that we're not in them. I meant to pay close attention, to notice, to see, to hear, to keep, always to keep: David, throwing at the target he drew on the garage door for hours until he got it right; Cathy, carrying her basket jungle with the little model dinosaurs and the artificial grass from some old Easter egg hunt and the genuine celery stalks for trees; Mindy, practicing with her violin, standing on one leg, her other crooked, the foot resting against the upright knee, playing those unbearably beautiful bars of the second movement from Mozart's Third Violin Concerto. What if my memory of what things were and where they were turns out to be as faulty as it is in most matters? When I left my office on campus, the route took me south across Bellaire Drive North and along one block of Wabash Street, then angling across Berry Street and down the long block on Odessa Street, and then I turned right on Devitt and into the driveway and through the garage (I never fixed the floor), and onto the screened-in porch that connected the garage and the house. The grill I used for cooking was there, and the dryer and the freezer and a set of shelves and a blue table and a red table, and the door into the kitchen. I remember the house. I believe I remember it well. I hope I remember it well.

Except, of course, that my memory is not like another's. Another's memory, different from mine, makes the place real, and another's, and another's, and another's. I cannot catch them all. A place is real, somehow, in its physical situation and in my memory, but I cannot catch all the memories of it. Where there is a real place, whole with the memories of it, I might be real, too. If I could know the past, I might be in the present. I must always lack the other's knowledge: I *must* be nostalgic. If I read a novel in the linear way, I miss the *other*, the geography of spatial relationships. In the name of God, why wouldn't you look for a past, a home, a place?

Inevitable and omnipresent as I believe it is, nostalgia as often as not hides, disguises itself, masks itself as altogether otherwise. We are nostalgics, even if unaware. In our best, most insistent greed and in our most longing, most desperate, and sometimes dumbest quests for authority, in whatever form we want it to take, we are looking for home, for the sure place, where identity is accepted and assured. We are looking for that other time, where change is not always making the world come undone. Diverse analysts, psychologists, and psychotherapists have matters quite upside down. Our greed and our search for authority do not take us toward metaphors for the womb. Hardly anyone wants, or ever wanted, even figuratively, even in dark dreams, to climb back up that tight channel to that place without identity. The womb is the metaphor, not the goal. We are mostly human and often adult: we look at that other time, and we know that it was an actual rural setting, not a figurative womb, where change, though not nonexistent, was slow and maybe didn't rush us every moment into the melancholy that always comes after change and grows more woeful later. Or perhaps it's only the otherness we can't know. Nostalgia might be as much in the future as in the past tense, at least in our saner moments. Our moments are not always sane; then, the ache always takes us backward, though seldom to real places.

In the late twentieth century, for example, much of our agitation for educational reform has urged us toward an imagined past, not toward an imagined future.

In olden days, when John Wayne rode tall in the saddle, the cavalry mostly came to save the settlers from their despair, throwing the barbarians back and saving another corner of the world for WASPish civilization as proclaimed and practiced in some mythical mid-American place during an unidentified but presumably no less real Golden Age. Now that world seems gone. Now sadness comes down, and no trumpets sound — at least it seems so among the circled wagons of those who comment on the perilous circumstances of education.

A profound nostalgia, a pain, a keening wail of loss afflict many commentators on higher education. They are besieged or already overrun, they seem to have lost what gave them hope, and they wait for the cavalry to come and rescue a world that probably never was.

I cannot claim that such lamentations are universal. They surely are not; at any rate, I have not counted. The litany of loss, pain, and nostalgia is, however, a common chorus, though I must say that even if it occurred only infrequently, that would be enough to arouse some fretfulness about the future of education. Things are not as they were formerly, and we grieve. We want authority. We want an official body of knowledge (which means an official body of doctrine). Very little agreement exists, *Time* tells us, on what students are learning or should be learning, and we aren't quite sure whether or not there is such a thing as a community of educated men and women. "The traditional curriculum, such as it was," *Time* reports, "virtually disintegrated during the campus upheavals of the 1960s. . . . [Now,] while educators reorganize their methods, the fundamental goals of the process — truth, knowledge, the understanding of the world — remain somewhere just beyond the horizon."

And what do we do? Too often, we hope the cavalry will come.

Too often, we yearn for an authority, however it is named, to save us. One commentator hopes to find a "consensual view" that will save us. Another weeps that we have no coherent philosophy. Another says that universities no longer work under the authority of a moral purpose. Another decries the absence of a unifying principle. Required courses, another says, reveal a "staggering incoherence of purpose." Another seems to believe that we are lost in the search for a definition of quality. Still another believes that we "lack a clear voice of authority." Another wants "a new authority." Another explains that education has deteriorated and that we need "a new consensus." Others appear to believe in some "official" body of knowledge and skills, which they are likely to call "the Great Tradition."

All educational good, we fear, is elsewhere, maybe lost, and nostalgia becomes a normal mode of educational commentary. The nostalgic need to "get back to the basics" — or wherever — emerges from a large unease, a marked uncertainty, a sharp dismay, and many grave doubts about our institutions. We're already living in a new world, and it took strange shape around us before we were ready. We look at this new world and raise a keening cry for the great otherwise. We forget that we have nowhere save ourselves to look for valor.

In this setting, it is not surprising that new saints should come to save us, come to be official voices of our nostalgia. It would have been surprising if Allan Bloom, E. D. Hirsch, Jr., and William Bennett had *not* come along to evangelize among us, to be among the most popular of what the editor of *Daedalus* calls our "merchants of nostalgia."

I won't be able to prove here that nostalgia is a continuous human condition, though usually disguised. Still, I think, diverse forms of human thought, ambition, and behavior, when unmasked, reveal themselves as versions of nostalgia.

Freud, Michael Vincent Miller observes, "made a tortured nostalgia the central mode of consciousness for representing incestuous passions." That may be upside down, of course, the incestuous passion being a metaphorical management — except to victims — of a tortured and persistent nostalgia. And is it possible that the rising, or more fully revealed, figures for child abuse evince not a need for sexual release or power or control, but for (momentary) ease from the nostalgic ache?

If Carl Jung had an affair with his patient, or if John Kennedy messed around, we are angry at the supposed loss of prophet or leader, but more particularly at the new blemishes on that scene of our innocence and expectation elsewhere. In the Edens we compose, no one is supposed to fuck unless we have already authorized it.

But it does happen. Many of those born before World War II reckon that it may have happened even more than they suspect, and they are angry at the "sexual revolution"; indeed, they are mad that the 1960s ever occurred, and now in the reactionary 1980s and after do what they can to erase a decade from our history and make us innocent again, longing not for personal responsibility but for the immutable moral design of a dear elsewhere, if not for puritanism, then for a sweet world that never existed except, perhaps, in the movies of the 1930s and 1940s. It all went to hell, they think, and now, as Elizabeth Hardwick puts it, "You cannot seduce anyone when innocence is not a value." They think. We think. Everywhere we long for sites of significance, scenes where we exist as we thought we did. The scenes are gone, and we're not there.

Can we doubt anymore that we live in the long later time after great change? Change is always great, and we're always trying to fix an unfixed world. We are not what we were a moment ago, and we long for the sweet *was* that went before or elsewhere or may come yet.

Some believe that nostalgia, too, is already gone. In her essay "Midwestern Poetry: Goodbye to All That," Lisel Mueller remarks,

> Poets from the Midwest tend to be specific: they write of
> the disappearance of the countryside, of tottering farmhouses
> with broken windows, of highways and shopping centers
> and parking lots that once were villages, but what they are
> mourning, of course, is the exhaustion of a distinct culture.

Among the middle-aged poets—and this is the generation I have been discussing—nostalgia is strong. But for a poet as young as James Tate, born in 1943 in Kansas City, Missouri, it is already too late for nostalgia. He can remember only the breakup; the roots that are still attached to him have lost their purpose, like outworn evolutionary appendages. His poems are full of restlessness, loneliness, a sense of blind alleys; places appear to be formless; human shapes have no substance. The old order is gone: where there was a center, there is a vacuum; where there was stability, there is flux; consumer conformity has taken the place of shared beliefs.

Perhaps so, but I think not. I think the condition she describes in the work of the young poet *is* one of our versions of nostalgia. Nostalgia is inevitable, though it takes many forms. We became nostalgic when we became self-conscious. That happens at various times for individuals; for the Western world it seems to have happened at least in the early Renaissance. Now, self-conscious, therefore nostalgic, we are born to remember, even if what we're trying to remember has not yet transpired. In an essay titled "History and the Ache of Time," Robert L. Tyler observes that "the knowledge of 'actual' as opposed to 'mythic' history constitutes a kind of irreversible expulsion from Eden." And so we remember.

What we remember is not always what happened and not always momentous. I remember an easy chair mashed to my specifications, another chair, a typewriter. I remember a rib steak with a crust of crushed peppercorns, and green beans and black-eyed peas and okra from the garden. I remember cheesecake and hamburgers and roast with Yorkshire pudding. Youth, belongings, the signs of our own identities, the scenes of what we imagined were our own geography—all may go to hell, disappear, and we remember, sometimes remember what was not but may be elsewhere or hereafter. Even Rhett Butler knew that the days that are gone seem to have a "genial grace." Even where we do not grieve for loss itself, we are saddened by the sense of loss, the idea of loss.

We know nostalgia best, to be sure, as the ache for a lost home. Not all homes are actual, and not all are lost. The ache for home, however, is always actual, even if we do not know a *topos* to long for, to love, except perhaps what Gaston Bachelard calls "felicitous space." Much as we may want to be citizens of the world, the world is too large for our love. We believe we remember, or we hunt for, the dear elsewhere, which will be somehow beyond the anxiety of the human condition and smaller than earth. This I judge to be normal behavior, though it can go haywire in uncertainty—neurotic behavior is not different from, but an excess of, normal behavior. John Herbers suggests in *The New Heartland* that attacks against abortion and textbooks and secular humanism and the defeat of the Equal Rights Amendment are versions of the great longing for the beautiful home that was, that wasn't.

I won't be able to prove that nostalgia is a continuous human condition, and I won't be able to be surprised when others take nostalgia differently, as Janice Doane and Devon Hodges do in *Nostalgia and Sexual Difference*, though I applaud their approach:

Nostalgia: *nostos;* the return home. Nostalgia permeates American politics and mass culture. While pulpits and podiums resound with the message that we need to restore American values and the American family, movies and television return us to the happy days of yore. This book explores a particular aspect of the contemporary effort to redeem an idealized past. As feminists, we argue that nostalgic writers construct their visions of a golden past to authenticate woman's traditional place and to challenge the outspoken feminist criticisms of it. *Nostalgia* is not just a sentiment but also a rhetorical practice. In the imaginative past of nostalgic writers, men were men, women were women, and reality was real. To retrieve "reality," an authentic language, and "natural" sexual identity, these writers fight the false, seductive images of a decadent culture that they believe are promoted by feminist writing. The battleground is representation itself: feminism is envisioned as a source of degenerate writing that threatens male authority. At issue are basic questions about the authority of women's writing and the power of male discourse to define reality.

The Ache for Home 159

Now that I think about it, I think that they and I are not so far apart, except, of course, that I would not call nostalgia either merely a sentiment or only a rhetorical practice, but a constant in human behavior—here, in the book by Doane and Hodges, turned to particular uses. Women are lonesome for themselves; they ache for the scenes of their own significance, the sites of their identity undefined by males.

Marilynne Robinson, in "Writers and the Nostalgic Fallacy," speaks of the "tired assumptions we try to build on and the cumbered and self-referential language we use that keep us in a narrow space, lamenting":

> the words, the images, associated with contemporary life are tendentious because, while we have no sense of history, we are enchanted by a myth of history, a truly venerable fable, which goes like this: Once the world was as it ought to be, then came the Catastrophe, after which we have toiled in twilight, lost and downcast. No one knows how old that story is, but it has never been more passionately believed than it is now.
>
> The Golden Age can be prehistoric, Classical, medieval, third world, or European, or American in any previous era, or it need no longer be invoked at all. The Catastrophe can be situated between any present moment and any other whose imputed qualities mark it as prelapsarian.

I will not be able to prove that we are perpetually nostalgic, though I believe we are. I believe that nostalgia is not part of an ancient story only, not simply a tired assumption, but a persistence not yet fully recognized in the human condition. The catastrophe always happens between this moment and the last. We're always trying to tell ourselves and others where our place is or was or will be, as Frederick Garber observes in "Geographies and Languages and Selves and What They Do."

> Texts are places where selves dwell, home-places for the self. Selves occupy texts the way Thoreau occupied Emerson's land, the way Wordsworth occupied Grasmere, the way Wil-

liams occupied Paterson and Stevens the Florida Keys. A good deal follows from this, including an odd interchangeability of self, place and text. For one thing, one of the ways the self gets to be at home in the world is through the fashioning of geographies, exploring and mapping places and then making homes within them. But if texts can be seen as places then the making of a text is itself a kind of geographizing, an act of self-locating, a mapping-out of linguistic spaces within which the self can dwell. All of which is to say that self, place and text define and determine each other, each the others' maker in a play that never ceases.

That's true, and not true. Once they become "home-places for the self," they cease being home-places for the self. The text—whether it is a poem, a novel, a case report at the office, a story told to a friend over coffee at the kitchen table, or a huge history—once it is told, already indeed in being told, may indeed be a home-place for the self, but it also departs into the consciousness, memory, interpretive capacity of the other, and is gone. Gone. Then once again, as Chesterton put it, we are "homesick at home." I will always lack the other's knowledge: I *must* be nostalgic, and so must we all. Nostalgia is a constant human condition.

But nostalgia does not come upon us singly. It is always with us in the presence of other events and forces. Nostalgia is always accompanied by a conflict of tongues, by the failure of memory, and by the threat of personal invisibility. And there is more: we always come into this world educated in the wrong curriculum. None of these is the cause of the others or the result of the others. They accompany each other, always in the presence of each other. If there is a cause, it is change itself, and there is always great change: the world always comes unfixed, and we're always having to try to fix it.

22

When Rhetorics Collide

Before everything happens, as everything happens, after everything happens, nostalgia waits and memory fails.

There, in inescapable nostalgia, with memory failing, we live perpetually among competing and colliding rhetorics.

Not long ago I went to Frankelberger's across the street to have a hot dog. They make good hot dogs. I watched a family across the room—a woman, a man, their two sons. The man had a fat belly and skinny legs (he was wearing shorts, in case you wondered), but otherwise I judge that he was in his own mind at least a risen John Wayne, a true old tiger. He spoke with a voice of resonant though mostly useless authority, and he beckoned with an imperious finger. His wife, at his command, took the two boys to the rest room, serially. She rose at his beckoning to fetch him condiments for his hamburger. He was a pig.

But I was sitting too far away to know him. Another could know him in better ways, sitting nearer; and even if it turned out that he really is a pig, likely he's a pig with his own character, his own way of being in the world, and that ought to be told. He should not be left to my distant view. If we don't know how to tell his way of being in the world, we can move up closer, learn, catch him for a moment, say his name, tell his habituations, celebrate his quirks.

Anything, I'm trying to say, and to tell myself, may yield delight, insight, wisdom, guidance when seen at the right distance; anything may even be dear. That includes literary theorists, literary critics, and poets I am presently disposed to dislike, distrust, and disapprove. It probably even includes television sports announcers and Republicans. That pig in the restaurant, well perceived, probably incorporates and thereby reveals to us a particular kind of culture and is therefore valuable, if for no other reason.

That doesn't mean that I want to spend a lot of time visiting with him. He had already become his authority, and I had already decided to disapprove. We didn't collide, except in my mind, but I was already superior, and he was already an ass. Authorities — potential tyrants — come, of course, in diverse wondrous shapes: the great theorist, the master philosopher, the dominant fashion maker–trendsetter, the current poet, the "in" style. No day passes without our elevation of texts, toys, or totems to positions of holiness; the same rules that allow us to talk about them in respectful tones enable us to make mean judgments about the other's texts, toys, or totems.

The arenas where rhetorics compete and collide seem to be prime breeding grounds for authorities, chiefs, and mandarins, some of them waiting to be tyrants. Sometimes, there, we pull off a small miracle and make a little joy.

Mostly we don't. We are commonly apart, perhaps even happily, and pretty well accustomed to separations among our discourses, sometimes not even noticing that we do not know each other. I really don't want us all to agree, to be a system-bound tribe. I don't want us to surrender to authority, though we do, choosing tyrants from among the fashions, ideas, and texts around us, privileging one above the other, making some tyrant's path all the easier as we accept another's thought and word without doing our homework. Ordinarily, doing our homework is a stay against being owned.

But it doesn't always work. Privileging behavior occurs in many ways and sometimes seems, perhaps is, inescapable. A colleague down the hall praises fiction over nonfiction. The one is called "creative"; the other, I suppose, is therefore "not creative" and by definition is devalorized. I read new composition textbooks and see that time after time, all best intentions notwithstanding, they teach argument as a form of self-valorization in which arguments are "presented" and evidence is "displayed" over against the other. I listen as colleagues prize "the giants of our literary tradition" above the poor, puny voice of the citizen. That's idol worship, I'd say, while remembering that the most famous fellow who spoke against idol worship didn't make it into the Promised Land. Or I read, for these past fifteen years, about the "back to the basics" movement and think how interesting it is that most of those who want to get back to the basics in our schools seem to believe that the last manifestation of the basics occurred at the same time they were in school. After them, the collapse of all standards. Standards gone, we hunt a new authority and make a best-seller of *The Closing of the American Mind*, granting ownership of ourselves to someone else.

Still, if I profess to be angry at those who *own*, whether ownership is conferred on them by others or usurped by themselves, if I am angry at those who accept or take privilege, that entails being angry at myself: by speaking as I have been speaking, I privilege my own views.

The man with the hamburger comes belatedly back to my mind. I reckon that we have every reason to hunt each other. In every rhetorical transaction—and *all* transactions are rhetorical—there are *always* competing rhetorics, first one, then the other, each expanding at the cost of the other's diminution.

The notion of multiple rhetorics should not be alien to us. They are all around us and inside us. The Left will not talk as the Right talks. The Baptist will not make the same speech that the Catholic makes. The woman will probably not talk as the man talks. The conscious mind and the subconscious will shape experience differently. The man who believes he was born in sin and continuously damned thereafter will not use language in the same way that a woman will who believes she was born innocent or good with every possibility of better yet to come. The first can at best only use words to try *to recover* from his own limitations. The second, however, may be free to use words *to reveal* her own present character.

I read on microfilm the surviving issues from 1934 through 1945 of the *Jayton Chronicle*, a weekly newspaper in West Texas. My microfilm contains 241 issues of the paper, or a little over a third of the total number of issues that would have been published in those twelve years. I read and take notes. I discover things that I didn't know and things I thought I knew well but had wrong or misremembered or misinterpreted; I learn about places where I should have been but wasn't, places where I shouldn't have been but was. I read and take notes, and I write my version of those years, and my version begins to take over, to expand, and to become the rhetoric of the occasion, compressing the *Jayton Chronicle* to my uses. I make my rhetoric out of the 241 issues, trying to forget that almost two-thirds of the issues are missing, apparently gone forever, writing without knowing what was in the missing papers. Can I ever know *just* what the other knows, or is?

By the time another rhetoric reaches us, we may already have changed it. Brains, I'm told, contain what have been called "feature detectors," specialized cell groupings that filter reality by responding only to some stimuli. Or stimuli get in—announcing themselves, say, through the eye—but the brain decides not to believe the current news and rearranges what the eye had seen. Perhaps I'll never know *just* what the other knows, or is.

I read an essay written by a young man in my class. It has already been compressed: out of his living time it has been compressed into his composing time and then into my reading time. There, though it has been compressed, it wants to expand and, at least temporarily, to take over my reading time, then my judgment. Sometimes I resist. It's hard to read him amidst all that clutter.

Colliding and competing rhetorics occur wherever two or more discourses—no matter how casual or how intense—encounter each other to compress or to expand.

But it doesn't take two to tango. Or to compete. Every soul carries competing rhetorics. I am often if not always at war. Habit wars with new vision. Ambition wars with laziness. The need to search out new country wars with the need to lean back and know the old. Pride wars with the realization that there is no occasion for pride. I send conflicting messages to myself and to others. I deceive myself. After a while and once in a while, you have to find a place where you can speak for the self; in that place you have to be infallible, even if it's only for a moment, even if it's a public pose, not a private reality, else you die of your own insignificance, have to speak infallibly against your own uncertainty. And, if we're reasonably healthy, infallibility must after a while give way to uncertainty. Uncertainty and infallibility pulsate against each other. Each of us is a gathering place for a host of rhetorical universes. Some of them we inhabit alone, and some of them we occupy without knowing that we do so. Each of us is a busy corner where multiple rhetorical universes intersect. Each of us is a cosmos. All rhetorical universes are still present. The debris of all our generations is always around us and in us. Sometimes they cross or try to mix. Sometimes we don't remember them well or keep order among them. Each of us is a crowd. Into this gathering — diverse personal rhetorics, culture rhetorics, folk rhetorics, family rhetorics, emotional rhetorics, physiological rhetorics, and on, and on — uncertainty and change keep introducing disorder. We always have to be making the world; its continual unmaking will continually undo us. When rhetorics collide, think of the residues that fall out but will not rest, the whispers that don't subside but persist, the dominations and subordinations that occur. Think of all you didn't say that time but wanted to. Think of all we might have said together but didn't. Think of the worlds we might have made.

Not all encounters and collisions involve a good rhetoric and a bad rhetoric or a powerful rhetoric and a weak rhetoric. Most of us spend most of our lives among contending internal and external rhetorics in which the issue is not clear and may not even be momentous, though it will determine the course of lives. Some collisions are gentle enough. School is a series of collisions. We probably learn in collisions. Some are not gentle.

I've been told that dogs — or maybe it was cats — are color-blind. They see shapes quickly, I was given to understand, and they see gradations of light and dark, but not color. I don't know that this is true; my source was a friend who sometimes decorates the truth. No dog — or cat, as the case may be — has said anything to me about the matter. If it is true, it doesn't appear to handicap them much. They seem able to find food fast enough. The last dog I knew was as fast as any, and faster than most, at locating food. If someone drove by the house in a car with the windows rolled up and a hamburger wrapped up inside a sack, she was at the table sitting up with her fork in her hand before the car turned the next corner. I'm not color-blind, but I don't think I have a particularly sharp eye for distinguishing among tones and shades of color. I don't know whether this is a consequence of incapacity or inattention. I do know that I have not seen colors that other people have seen. For example, three people have told me that my hair is red. The three do not include my father and my mother, and you'd think they would know. One time when I was young, I asked my father what color my hair was. He said that he had never noticed. I also asked my mother, and she reported that it was "sort of a turd-muckledy dun." Whatever the case when I was young, my hair is clearly not red now, as I am able to see things. In its present manifestation, part of my hair is bald-colored. Part of it is gray. Part of it is white. A few strands are soiled blond. Most of what's left, I think, is pretty much the color of sand, but not a very high quality sand. I'm pretty sure that it never was red, but three people I've known, all pretty astute in other respects, told me it was. One of them was a lady I worked with, now long gone, though stories about her still whisper through the halls. I never questioned her about her perception of my hair, and she was not given to doubting herself. The other two were Aunt Edith and Aunt Bill. I could tell you why Aunt Bill was called Bill, but that's another story. They were the most elegant and refined of my aunts. I'm not denying the elegance and refinement of my other aunts, but in each of them other qualities seemed to come first. Aunt Nell could outwrestle all of her nephews, serially or simultaneously. Aunt Cora couldn't wrestle much, but she could intimidate us. I was a little afraid of Aunt Mary, and I never did seem to know Aunt Lizzie very well. At any rate, I never thought to question Aunt Edith and Aunt Bill when they said my hair was red. It would have been boorish to do so, though I didn't know that word in my early days. People see red for their own reasons, I guess. In the instance of my hair, that creates no problem. Sometimes I don't much like the reasons people have for seeing red. In the early 1950s a lot of people in this country took to seeing Red everywhere. They were encouraged in this by Senator Joseph McCarthy, who went about the country slaying Reds (by his definition) with the jawbone of an ass (his own). Some people see red easily because in arrogance or ignorance or dogma they are always entirely convinced that they are absolutely right, and so they get mad at all the other people who are absolutely wrong, or maybe heretical. It wasn't so with my colleague, now gone, and my two aunts. They saw red because they saw red. I don't see the red they saw, but I don't have to, and they didn't have to see what I saw. We live in the world in different ways, and the colors one person sees aren't the colors another sees. Mostly, that's a pretty good arrangement.

Some collisions seem gentle enough but aren't, have instead the force to change a nation. Television, for example, routinely diverts us with rapidly shifting programs, on the one hand, and instructs us, on the other, with insistent, repeated, fixed images. If television is injurious to our psyches, I'd reckon that the effect occurs in quieter ways than we have imagined. Sex and violence on television probably have a more limited effect on us than the quieter instruction in our culture that shows on the screen almost all of the time. To suppose that television does not affect us is to claim that experience has no consequence. Anything else we do for thirty-one and a half hours a week (a recent figure for average individual viewing) would have some effect on us. As Michael Novak points out, jogging that much a week, or writing or working or reading, would modify the way we think and take the world. Novak also remarks that "television is a molder of the soul's geography," that it now "constitutes a major source of guidance for behavior." One way the medium does this is in its mixture of verbal and visual messages. Television is an apparently single medium that is always carrying at least two messages, one sometimes spoken and pictured, the other always silent but pictured. Verbal messages shout, then pass on, but the landscape remains the same. What's depicted in the wholly visual background/setting/landscape is a pretty stable world. This scene provides the background, the rhythms, the assumptions by which we live, try to live, or think we should live. This scene, I'd suggest, enters our lives so constantly and so deeply that we often don't acknowledge it: it becomes part of a secular liturgy for our lives. And what are these repeated images? What is this life like? What does it tell us to be like? They are images of affluence. They depict a white world, Bill Cosby notwithstanding. They depict a largely male world, a sex-driven world, with a majority of the images emerging from sexually charged atmospheres. They depict a world that is within reach of probably fewer than 10 percent of the viewers, but against which they must nevertheless be measured. They picture a world that is relatively uncomplex, focusing on a rather narrow range of human emotions and motives. Their effect is to homogenize. Television does not favor the varieties of accent and speech and other cultural differences that can be found in our country. Television does not favor places; it is a land that is no land. When we go into that land, we are delivered to the culture and its advertisers, and we don't even have to remember specific advertisements—we remember the repeated images of the right world and its brand names. The stable visual image teaches us how to be in the world.

Sometimes the collisions kill us. In the opening moments of Leni Riefenstahl's *The Triumph of the Will*, a newly authorized rhetoric arrives. An airplane bearing Adolph Hitler to a 1934 party rally descends out of the clouds over Nuremberg. The camera follows the plane on its descent, and the plane has about it the character of both the eagle of Nazi heraldry and the chariot of the new Messiah. The German people had what they deemed a great, hurting need, and he came forward as the one uniquely able to fulfill their need. Questions of truth and consistency came to be relatively unimportant. Hitler created an image of himself as the embodiment of the mission and hope of the Germans. He was *the* one, sure of himself, never in doubt. After the invasion of the Rhineland he said of himself, "Anyone other than myself would have lost his nerve." He and the party brought the people into their "siege drama" as performers in a new liturgy, and soon all opposing voices were silenced, and soon European Jews began to disappear and to die. Propagandists said they bore filth and disease; they were germ-carriers; they had about them a ferment of decomposition. Even among the educated, as Lucy Dawidowicz reminded us, there sounded over and over again the refrain, "Die Juden sind unser Unglüch." The people, Hitler wrote in *Mein Kampf*, would believe anything if it were sufficiently repeated. Language became, in new secular liturgy, the carrier of poison. Over and over the liturgy was repeated throughout Germany:

EIN REICH, EIN VOLK, EIN FÜHRER, or DAS REICH IST DER FÜHRER, or worse, DEUTSCHLAND ERWACHE, JUDA VERRECKE; DEUTSCHLAND ERWACHE, JUDA VERRECKE. The unspeakable was said over and over for twelve years, and a rhetoric destroyed humanness, elevated bestiality.

We are the rhetoric over against others, and they against us. We live in, through, around, and against arguments. What happens if the story of another crushes up against our own—disruptive, shocking, incomprehensible, threatening, suddenly showing us a narrative not our own? What happens if a narrative was lacking all along, though it is the only evidence of our identity? Do we hold onto our rhetoric, keep telling the story we have been telling all along? At all costs? We react, of course, in many different ways. Sometimes we turn away from other narratives. Sometimes we teach ourselves not to know that there are other narratives. Some-times—probably all too seldom—we encounter another narrative and learn to change our own. Sometimes we lose our plot, and our convictions as well; since our convictions belong to our nar-ratives, any strong interference with our narrative or sapping of its way of being will also interrupt or sap our convictions. Sometimes we go to war. Sometimes we sink into madness, totally unable to manage what our wit or judgment has shown us—a contending narrative that has force to it and charm and appeal and perhaps justice and beauty as well, a narrative compelling us to attention and toward belief that we ultimately give, a contending narrative that shakes and cracks all foundations and promises to alter our identity, a narrative that would educate us to be wholly other than what we are. Any narrative exists in time; any narrative is made of the past, the present, and the future. We cannot without poten-tial harm shift from the past of one narrative into the present and future of another, or from the past and present of one narra-tive into the future of or from the future we are narrating into a past that is not readily ours. And what if both parties are entirely steadfast, wholly intent on preserving the nature and movement of their rhetorics, earnest and zealous to keep their identities? And what if they come together in a setting in which contention generates a flushed, feverish, quaky, shaky, angry, scared, hurt, shocked, disappointed, alarmed, outraged, even terrified condition? I mean such occasions as these: let two people confront each other, each holding views antithetical to the sacred values and images of the other, one an extreme advocate of the current pro-life movement, the other an extreme advocate of the current movement to leave free choice open to women in the matter of abortion, each a mockery of the other; let two parties confront each other, zealous advocates of one contending that farmers must learn to stand on their own without government support, and zealous advocates of the other contending that the government, by withdrawing support, will literally kill farmers; let two tribes go to war for ancient reasons not entirely explicable to themselves or to outsiders, each a denial of the other, as in various current Middle East crises; let two nations confront each other in what sometimes appears to be a shocked and total inability to understand or even to recognize each other, as in continuing conflicts between the United States and Russia, wherever these conflicts happen to be located, whether in East Germany or Nicaragua; let a beautiful Jewish woman encounter an aged captain of guards for Dachau; let some man confront an affirmation of life he has not been able to achieve; let an honest woman encounter cruel dishonesty; let a man encounter a narrative so beautiful but different that he cannot look; let two quite different narratives converge in conflict inside the head of a single lonely man or woman. We are the rhetorics against each other.

The collision of rhetorics *is* change; change *is* the collision of rhetorics.

Change always occurs. This moment gives way to the next.

Change doesn't have to come upon us from without. We always create it from within. I have looked at the Double Mountains all my life, but I have never seen them: through refraction I always misinterpret their color; through distance cues I always misinterpret their size. I always knew my mother and my father, but never knew them as I might. In change/collision, some rhetorics appear to be lost, but most persist. Lost rhetorics, indeed, are never lost. They pulsate against the present, and even in the present we are always in lost rhetorics—always nostalgic—trying to speak into a new world from a gone world. The residues left from the competition of rhetorics, the ghosts, whispers, echoes, never go away. We hear them.

We are inevitably nostalgic. Nostalgia, the ache for home, is a perpetual human condition, even if it's disguised as greed, educational reform, sexual longing, or the need for authority. What was is always contending with what is; what is elsewhere is always contending with what is here: we're always in competing rhetorics.

There — nostalgic among competing rhetorics — memory always fails us. We can never find exactly who we were or whatever might have been. Whoever we were and whatever might have been have already been lost to us in the transformations of compressing and expanding rhetorics.

There — nostalgic among competing rhetorics with failing memory — I'm always on the point of disappearing. As it is always possible for me to be compressed, perhaps to nothing, as it is always possible for nostalgia to lose me elsewhere, as I cannot depend on memory to recall who I am, invisibility is always imminent, especially in the presence of all those others who seem to know, who seem to know both text and territory.

Can there be any doubt? My memory is not another's. Another's memory makes a place, an event, or an idea real, together with another's and another's. I can't catch them all. A place, an event, an idea is real in its situation *and* in all the memories and perceptions there are of it. I may even be able to see place, event, idea in its situation and in my memory, but I cannot catch all the other memories and perceptions of it. *I must always lack the other's knowledge. I must be nostalgic*, caught in competing rhetorics with memory failing, invisibility *imminent*.

I believe that there is still occasion for joy in our talking and writing, if we can once in a while pull off a small miracle. That's not easy: most of us aren't good enough writers to be clear to each other, or interesting; some of what passes for awesome complexity in writing is unfinished thought arrogantly presented as poetry or philosophy. We are already mysteries to each other: we slide off into lost rhetorics that aren't lost, careen off from rhetorics compressed and diminished or expanded beyond recognition. If we're to know each other from rhetoric to rhetoric, we're probably going to have to risk showing each other our lives; not pronouncing toward each other, but revealing whole structures of meaning that tell how we worked our way out of and through our past, choosing and not choosing, making a shape and style that give residence to meaning. Sometimes we can't do that—we're not good enough writers. Sometimes we'll choose not to—and that's a great freedom we must have. Sometimes, though, we might manage to live in our own voices, create our own geographies, yet inhabit them not as owners but as sharecroppers.

And then no place is ours, and we can't find it anyway, for memory has already failed.

23

Speak, Memory

Memory always fails. Memory always fails, and "there are no experts on memory's transformation / of landscape," Mark Doty writes, "or the recollection / of summers' amusements."

What happened just there? Just then? Did I know who I was then, before? Do I know now who I was then?

Seems unlikely: observation is always insufficient, memory is always wrong.

Why didn't I keep notes? More? Better?

I wonder why I have come sometimes to imagine that nothing is real until it's said, written—and then it's inadequate or worse because it rests on insufficient observation and errant memory. Perhaps I'm only your basic, maybe even prototypical (oh, I like to think at least that) post-Gutenberg man: nothing exists until it exists on the page.

I have the wrong questions. NOT: Why didn't I keep notes? More? Better? BUT: Why didn't I look more closely? Keep track? Pay attention?

If I didn't, and I didn't, is there any way of knowing who I became since, if observation is always already insufficient and memory is always already wrong?

I have imagined, or wanted to imagine, or believed I imagined, that nothing related to me will count unless I get it severed from myself. If what I think I observed becomes a piece of writing, then it's all right to consider, but not so if it's just myself. That's a strange disclaimer on myself, that nothing has value until it gets to be no longer myself. Strange disclaimer, impossible of fulfillment: whatever I observe or remember or say or write is always myself, whoever was, whoever is, even if witness transforms it.

But I can't easily rid myself of that urgency to abstract from myself, to find a large truth out there in the small particular I've known. Has my little migration been a version of the *volkswan-*

derung? Do my losses make a little holocaust? If there's any truth out there somewhere or in here, it's in the character of the small particulars, and I didn't keep notes enough, it may be, to tell for sure. How in the hell am I supposed to know what to make of all this if I didn't see it or, seeing, remember? If I don't know what I've left out?

Memory won't keep what we were, won't hold all the things that were in the world with us. Why didn't I look more closely? Keep track? Pay attention? Keep notes more and better? The central character in Shirley Ann Grau's *The Keepers of the House* says,

> Funny how memory is. There are places—months and years even—when I cannot recall a thing. There are simply blank spots with nothing to fill them.
>
> And I have tried. Because somehow or other I convinced myself that if I could just remember—could have all the parts—I would understand. And even so I can't. I've lost it somewhere.

Memory always fails, yet we must remember so that experience will make some kind of sense. We remember, and we can't.

Some, of course, trust their memory; it is their way of domesticating the past. In a review of Studs Terkel's *The Good War*, Loudon Wainwright remarks:

> Inherent in all oral history, however persuasive the accounts that go into it, is a certain vagueness and imprecision, for it is based on memory—which sometimes acquires hindsight—and is shaped inevitably by feelings. We often recall only what we want or need to recall, and we can be surprised later by our own distortions of the past. Made up of the memories of its narrators ("I was in combat for six weeks," says one man, "but I can remember every hour, every minute of the whole 42 days"), "The Good War" sometimes leaves one with the feeling that he should be reading some other book at the same time, not necessarily for the correction of errors but so that the events reported by Mr. Terkel's people may be located more exactly in time, place and context.

Some believe that failure of memory is far more than personal. Bruce Duffy observes that "memory is our wound: Memory is what confounds and defeats us." But greater than the wound of memory is what seems the contemporary failure of memory, our mounting unwillingness or apparent inability to look long and carefully at our past.

Perhaps. At any rate, memory always fails, as Dabney Stuart says in "Facing Up":

> If you choose to return home by a route different
> From the one by which you departed, no one
> Will recognize you. It's likely no one
> Will recognize you anyway, given the crowded air
> And the way our memories blur and thicken.

Whatever happened out there, Jeffrey Harrison observes in his poem "Eminent Domain," we can't see it:

> They took my grandparents' land and flooded it
> to make a recreation area.
> I thought I'd be able to look down into the lake
> and see the farm down there: the silo,
> the yellow house, the shipwrecked barn,
> tobacco leaves still hanging from the rafters
> now swaying like seaweed.
>
> And memory too has put it underwater,
> everything wavering, obscured, a kind of
> liquid night, the sunlight turned to moonlight,

I have looked at the Double Mountains for fifty years and have never seen them.

Whatever would have been memory was already long since being made into narrative. I can't catch events as they were, and they weren't the first time. The brain is not a passive receiver of whatever happened; it is the active creator of memory. The world, already narrated, is prodded and shoved and re-created by my own inchoate world making its own designs, deciding however haphazardly on the beginning, middle, and end of its own narrative that will be revised another day. Your construction of me is myself against your past, but not myself. My construction of you is yourself against my past, but not yourself. Both of us may have occurred against another past that may actually have happened.

And what if my memory of times and places and people and myself is always as wrong as I know it sometimes is? When I went to the museum at Fort Concho and saw Lieutenant Chadbourne's artifacts, I remembered well enough his sword belt. It was meant to hang from his right shoulder to his left waist. In the middle, over his heart, there is a neat bullet hole. I remembered that part right, but I misreported the rest. For years I told my children and friends and passing strangers about my very first train ride, alone, from Gilpin to Jayton, carrying a sack of Grandma Durham's teacakes. Last year, in an old issue of the *Jayton Chronicle*, I learned that it wasn't my first train ride.

I have relied on memory for atonement, but now I doubt remembering. When memory fails, is there no atonement?

24

Disappearing

If you look for me on the mountain, I won't be there. If you look for me on Odessa Street or in my office or at the third bench along the sidewalk, I won't be there.

If you look for me in Galveston or in San Angelo or at Robber's Cave State Park, I won't be there.

If you look for me, I won't be there.

I'm disappearing.

Why wouldn't I disappear? Everyone disappears, and no one notices. Why wouldn't I disappear?

After great change, I can't count on knowing who I might turn out to be, if anyone.

If I turned out to be anyone after great change, then in the long later time that comes next, how would I know? I'd miss, never recognize whoever I was.

But it's unlikely, after all, that I'd turn out to be anyone.

In that long later time after great change, the losses whittle me away. They go, and I go. When the last of them has died, I'll long since have disappeared. They can't go without taking chunks, without taking whole versions of me away. If you take a layer of myself away every day or week or month, how soon am I gone? Soon.

If all the places change, then where would I be? If you look for me, I won't be there. If all the places change, then there is no place left to be. If there is no place left to be, then you can't find me, for I'm gone.

When I look toward home and ache for home, there is no home: it has already changed, disappeared, gone. And just which home would I look for, Friend? Hell, we already knew, is a sad place, an eternity of regret. But think how sad Heaven would be: in Heaven there is no beer, or home.

Even if last traces of me remain, will you see them? Will they be at all visible? Probably not. Seen by you out of your world, I am invisible. I might be, with luck, the direct object of your sentence, or the indirect object; more likely the object of your prepositions, more likely not in your sentences at all.

Suppose I trust to memory to catch it all, and myself? Memory is always wrong, and the people are gone, and the places are gone, and I can't see the competing rhetorics, and I am gone, and what's left to memory, supposing memory could remember?

I won't be in Spur or at Grandpa's farm, not even down by the windmill or alongside the railroad trestle. I won't be at Gilpin, and Gilpin is gone. I won't be in Jayton, not on the square, for the square is gone, not in the house west of the square, not in the house northeast of the square, not in the shotgun house on the south side of the square, not in the little house not far from the Big Rock Candy Mountain, not in the house by the Croton Breaks, or in the house at 1033 Cleckler, not in Coleman Barracks outside Mannheim, not in Heidelberg, not at 3253 Merida, not at 604 Parkview in Norman, Oklahoma, not on Stadium Drive, not in my office, not here, not there, or there, not even in my own text.

If you look for me in the administration building or in a notable office, upstairs, downstairs, I won't be there.

If you look for me on Odessa Street or in the public library, I won't be there, or under the oak tree by Clark Hall, or in Billy Miner's Saloon, though I might have been there for a moment once.

If you look for me in Galveston or in San Angelo or in Fort Davis State Park, I won't be there.

If you look for me on the mountain, I won't be there.

If you look for me on the Double Mountains, I won't be there.

25

I Am the Twentieth Century

But I can't be invisible: I have to stay and be the twentieth century, maybe all of it.

I was born in September 1929. Sometime, early on after I began to understand about years and dates, I remember wondering what it would be like to live into another century—wouldn't be out of the question, I remember thinking, just seventy-one years and I'd make it.

Now it's 1989, and no matter. Even if I live far into the new century, even if the new century gets here, with me or without, I won't be part of the new century. I'm already of the twentieth century. I am the twentieth century.

> Hear, oh hear, the night bird call.
> Soon, oh soon, the dark must fall.

Maybe Freud was my father. Is that a way to commence the twentieth century? Maybe so, though he needed Einstein and Heisenberg and Goedel for help, and I can't claim all of them. Maybe he was my father. He was here sometime, though probably not in season to sire me.

Still, you never know: he was crafty and sometimes wise, and might have done the job. On Mondays, I doubt it. He and my mother wouldn't have moved in the same circles. She probably wouldn't have consented. Besides, he smoked cigars and might have been her father, too, and she was chaste, whether by principle or poverty of choice. I'm no longer sure.

I got the genes remembered almost right. I inherited the maladies he invented as best I could, though failing, I'd guess, in some notable dark particulars.

But maybe the little girl from Texas wasn't my mother. Maybe I wasn't born. Maybe, too, I had to be invented. I had to be invented so the whole entire total twentieth century could enact its foolishness, find a place for its trivialities and, sometimes, sins.

If that is so, that makes necessity my mother.

If I'm to be visible, will there be a mark on my forehead to tell that I'm the one to enact the century's foolishness, make a place for its trivialities and, sometimes, sins? Strange that there wouldn't be a brand. Usually there isn't.

I didn't, at any rate, want to be invisible. I want to be seen, admired—oh, at the very least admired. Always becoming invisible, I need to be told that I exist; I require to be assured of my worth even when I am worthless, invisible. I learned the century's lessons well: I must be seen if I'm to exist; I am not authentic until advertised, not real unless I'm imaged in the media.

> Hear, oh hear, the night bird call.
> Soon, oh soon, the dark must fall.

I am the twentieth century. I have believed its messages, have sometimes even taught them to others. I have believed. I exemplify. I'm it. Freud got me out of necessity. Advertising taught me. School failed me. I imagined the century's sexual fantasies, except that I was never quite sure what they were and had trouble getting the scene set to start with, getting the cast of characters straight, remembering who did what just when with whom, though it was my duty to imagine them all. If a real person fucks you gladly, does that make you an authentic person? Advertising taught me. School failed me. Church condemned me—how could it not? I learned regret at age five and invisibility soon thereafter, though I'm not allowed to be invisible. Invisible, I must be visible: if you have no identity, how do you tell everybody that everything is just fine, that everything is going to be all right, that we're going to have what's left of this century?

I have believed the messages, have sometimes even taught them to others, gladly enough. I have learned that there is no "real world" out there, wholly separate from ourselves, wholly apart from our own thinking and language. We make the world we live in. Our eyes are not innocent: they see what they interpret, not a "real world" that was out there before eyes looked. "Nature" is not real world. Nelson Goodman writes in *Of Mind and Other Matters* that "we must obviously look for truth not in the relation of a version to something outside that it refers to but in characteristics of the version itself and its relationships to other versions." Jerome Bruner and Carol Fleisher Feldman, in a commentary on Goodman's work, observe that

> right versions are versions that are true in *some* world. It is a right version of the everyday geocentric world that the earth is at rest when we step off a moving bus, though in the world of modern physics it is also a right version that the earth is always moving. But just as there are many right versions, each true in some world, there are many worlds. Now we have a kind of correspondence theory of truth in which every right version has a world corresponding to it. But unlike the usual correspondence theory, this one permits conflicting alternative accounts because apparently conflicting versions may each be true in some world, and there are many worlds. Or as Goodman puts it, since "there are conflicting true versions and they cannot be true in the same world," there must be many worlds. These worlds do not occupy the same space or time. "In any world," he says, "there is only one Earth"; and the several worlds—the world into which we step off the bus and the world of the astronomers—do not risk collision in the same space or time.

Oh but they do try to occupy the same space and time. I have heard and believed: that one earth out there spinning in space and down there still beneath my feet, that one I thought I learned about from my mother and my father and my big brother and from Mrs. Fowler in the first grade and Miss Rice in the second grade and Miss Kinney in the third grade and Mrs. Jay in the fourth grade *always* comes racing out of space and up from beneath my feet on collision course with the worlds I've since learned to see. Multiple worlds and their rhetorics always collide somewhere. I have learned and believed. Humans, we'd thought and still think, create the world they inhabit both through their conscious activities and through their unconscious projections. We come to wonder whether we can ever establish securely the meaning or range of meaning of what we construct, whether world or text. When I compose a world, it must collide with others; in composing, I have excluded, and the excluded will not disappear; in composing, I have excluded worlds and parts of worlds that I made myself and worlds and parts of worlds that others have made. Any thought, any world, must be unsettled by the competing other.

I have believed the century's messages and have sometimes even taught them to others.

I don't philosophize: I *am* philosophy. I am the twentieth century.

Do you wish to understand the twentieth century? Watch me live.

Do you wish to discover and to understand its histories? Watch me live.

Do you wish to study how the Western world lost its last pastoral, rural connections and moved to the city? How the people live nomadically now in their diaspora, even when they stay in one place? Watch me live.

Do you wish to understand territoriality and war and destruction? I have persecuted spirits, though I haven't maimed bodies. Watch me live.

Do you wish to understand how the people of the century lost diverse centers of belief, lost authorities and authentications of their lives? How some long for them? How some do not want them? Watch me live.

Do you wish to understand how our measurements came to be relative, and what happened then? Watch me live.

Do you wish to understand how what we thought we were measuring got a little confused, too? Do you wish to understand the Uncertainty Principle? Watch me live.

Do you wish to understand how strange and confusing it is when a version of truth, a system of thought, or a mere person tries to locate self-authentication? Watch me live.

Do you wish to understand how, when language became problematic, we all became rhetorics? Watch me live.

I have believed the century's messages. I exemplify. I'm it. I am invisible but must remain here — visible, though fuzzy around the edges — to be the century. I must make the world, but I don't know how.

> Hear, oh hear, the night bird call.
> Soon, oh soon, the dark must fall.

I must make the world, but I don't know how: in all those schools, I took the wrong courses.

26

The Lux Radio Theater

Today is Monday, December 26, 1988. In the past four days, if I have counted right, the movie *It's a Wonderful Life* has been shown seven times on various TV channels. I may have missed some listings in the TV schedule. I didn't watch *It's a Wonderful Life* this time around, or the last. Perhaps I should have, and perhaps I should have paid close attention. I was supposed to be the twentieth century, and I wasn't ready. *It's a Wonderful Life* appears to be the Christmas movie for a world that still once in a while wants to look like a Norman Rockwell cover. It appears to have replaced *Miracle on 34th Street*. If I had watched, I might have been ready to do Christmas in the late twentieth century, might have known how good and proper folks behave, get things done.

If television is our tutor now—and the messages it sends aren't all that different from those wonderful "madcap" comedies and patriotic war movies and sentimental dramas of the 1930s and 1940s—then movies and radio were before, in the time when I thought I was growing up. I had my lessons from the Hollywood scripture, even if, as Molly Haskell says, "The moguls who built Hollywood—mostly Jews, mostly immigrants, mostly the sons of fathers who were failures, and most of them yearning to assimilate—created a fantasy America that was far cleverer, more glamorous and more adventurous than the WASP reality. It was an America in which social divisions could be closed, the rich could learn humility, the poor could rise, the illiterate could acquire knowledge and Jews could become unhyphenated Americans." I learned my lessons well, as Ronald Reagan did, as millions did, and have been shocked ever since that the world didn't work out Hollywood style.

I begin to think that I learned the wrong lessons.

But I learned those lessons well, I think; I was catechized by Ronald Colman.

Many of us, I guess, learned the same lessons. Joan Joffe Hall tells some of them in her poem "Romance and Capitalism at the Movies":

> To the child the movie is mysterious.
> Like magic, her mother
> always knows what will happen. "She slapped
> his face," the mother says, "but in the end
> they'll get married." Murders—
> the child wonders how she knows who did it.
> It seems fitting, the mother's like
> that with the icebox too, no use
> wiping up spilled milk. Does she
> have eyes in the back of her head? Can she see
> into a child's heart?
> One day at a school movie some kids whisper
> in the row behind. "Just wait,"
> a girl says, "that guy's gonna lose his money."
> And the child realizes it's not magic,
> not her mother, it's movies; if you see
> enough of them you can gaze right into
> the heroine's heart, her secret love for a brute.
> You learn what the everyday fails to teach,
> that love goes kiss-slap-kiss,
> the filthy rich go broke, and honest
> folk end up happy unless they're women
> and sacrifice makes them radiant.

But until I was about nine years old, that scripture was hard to find, harder to hold. Mostly, before I came to see movies often and then regularly, I took my lessons from another scripture, radio.

I've wondered ever since how much the course of my foolish life was set by "The Lux Radio Theater." I go to the university library half expecting Cecil B. DeMille to be as thick as Descartes and maybe Jesus in the card catalog, but I don't find much except casual references and brief mentions. Strange that a culture would not know its primary tutors, isn't it? The public library downtown does little better—if there were once many books about radio, they've mostly, I guess, been crowded off the shelves by movie books and TV books, if they're books. Strange, too, that a person would not have surer recollections about his own philosophical sources. I mostly remember being enthralled, lost in that world. I didn't even know then that the dramatizations were abbreviated— I thought they were real, though I only remember a few in particular, "Libel," "Jezebel," and oh, oh, "Wuthering Heights." I know that I made sure to get to the radio a few minutes before eight o'clock on Monday evenings—I think my family listened to "The Voice of Firestone" at seven-thirty, and besides, I wanted to be sure I didn't miss anything—and I was sometimes enthralled until nine o'clock. (Sometimes I remember something correctly: the *Fort Worth Star Telegram* "Radio Clock" for Monday, April 3, 1939, confirms the time.)

But I doubt that I justly blame or praise "Lux Radio Theater" for myself. I took my character, too, from "I Love a Mystery" and "Jack Armstrong" and "The Shadow"

> (Several years ago in the Orient, Cranston learned a strange and mysterious secret . . . the hypnotic power to cloud men's minds so they cannot see him. Cranston's friend and companion, the lovely Margot Lane, is the only person who knows to whom the voice of the invisible Shadow belongs.)

and "Dick Tracy" and "The Lone Ranger"

> (With his faithful Indian companion, Tonto, the daring and resourceful masked rider of the plains led the fight for law and order in the early western United States. Nowhere in the pages of history can one find a greater champion of justice. Return with us now to those thrilling days of yesteryear.)

and "Jack Armstrong, the All-American Boy"

> (Wave the flag for Hudson High, boys!
> Show them how we stand!
> Ever shall our team be champion,
> Known throughout the land!)

The Lux Radio Theater 187

and maybe, too, from "Major Bowe's Original Amateur Hour" and "Fred Waring and His Pennsylvanians" and Charlie McCarthy and John Charles Thomas and Archie of "Duffy's Tavern" and maybe, too, from Tom Mix's Lucky Horseshoe Nail Ring

> (Won't you try Wheaties?
> They're whole wheat with all of the bran.
> Won't you buy Wheaties?
> For wheat is the best food of man).

I don't, in fact, know where the lessons came from or who taught them, the wrong lessons, the right lessons that I forgot. I've always assumed that my mother was the chief author of scripture. I've always assumed that I learned most lessons at her knee, though the truth is that I don't remember when or if she actually enunciated them to me: don't lie (I've told so many lies that I can't recognize the truth; if I could, it would slide right off the page as I write); stay clean; try not to act like Poor White Trash; make no scenes; call no attention to yourself; prepare for grief. I've mostly stayed clean. Otherwise, the lessons didn't take, or I forgot, and I don't know exactly where or why I learned to honor pipe, tobacco, coffee, books, cheap wine, a good game of softball that lasts forever or until your knees give out; where or why I learned to believe my mother's axioms, even if she didn't say them; where or why I learned that I would someday go to hell. In T. R. Hummer's poem "Dogma: Pigmeat and Whiskey," the narrator tells of his grandfather's stories:

> Stories, stories: he told them to us,
>
> And we listened, the same ones again and again.
> God knows we were bored, but we remembered
> Things he never even said.

Mostly, the lessons didn't take, or I forgot. Others seem so sure: even now, an "inspirational" book announces that "all I ever really needed to know I learned in kindergarten." I expect we learned more and less there than we usually think. Brooks Haxton writes in "Recess" of the "rage I felt at seven":

> I was afraid
> Of how I felt, afraid to break the rules,
> Afraid to call attention to myself,
> Afraid of what Mrs. Rowell would say, what
> Other kids would think.

The wrong lessons stayed on. The right lessons were lost to memory. Who knows what to make of the teachers?

What did I learn from the scriptures and tutors? Wrong lessons that stayed. Right lessons, maybe, that I forgot. Good lessons, apparently, that I ignored altogether.

I thought I learned to be silent, to call no attention to myself, to make no scene. I was, I thought, part of what Fred E. H. Schroeder calls an "unwanted generation," born in 1929 and hungry in the years following, when food wasn't always easy to come by. I was intimidated by the generation just older, those who went heroically to war in 1941 and came back, somewhat fewer, to intimidate me again, returning to school just as I was starting to college in 1946, fresh, untested, unfinished. I thought I learned to be silent. That's a good lesson, and a bad lesson. I obeyed it at wrong times, rebelled against it at wrong times, was silent when I shouldn't have been, spoke when I might have been silent.

God help me, I may even have learned to love war. I may have learned that war is the last, the right and proper, testing ground. In a review of Elmer Bendiner's *The Fall of Fortresses*, Drew Middleton says:

> The centerpiece of "The Fall of Fortresses" is an account of the attack on Aug. 17, 1943, on the ball bearing works at Schweinfurt in the heart of Germany by 230 Forts of the First Bomb Wing. The German fighters and the American bombers fought one of the bloodiest air battles in history. The American losses incurred there and in an attack on the same day on Regensburg were 60 bombers, 600 men.
>
> Yet the sight of the mass of bombers taking off roused

Mr. Bendiner, who confesses nonetheless that his exultation was an "act of treason against the intellect, because I have seen dead men washed out of their turrets with a hose."

I remember straightening a little in parade when the band commenced that old cavalry tune "Garry Owen," just for us, the modern cavalry of the tank battalions. I remember a flutter down my back at retreat parade in early autumn, just outside Mannheim, when the battalion colors came by, the battle streamers pulled out behind by the wind. God, yes, I learned that old lesson, and it was always wrong.

Sometimes I think I learned everything wrong, though I always thought it was right, at least for a while. Ever so slowly in the last of the 1930s and the beginning of the 1940s, I thought I was beginning to catch on about "classical" music. One of my chief instructors, even if he didn't know it, was Arturo Toscanini with the NBC Symphony Orchestra. Now, just yesterday or so, I learn that Toscanini had already decided which music I should hear, which I shouldn't hear:

> By the time Toscanini and David Sarnoff of RCA were collaborating on the NBC orchestra, the maestro was 70 years old and he had pared down his repertory to a relatively small selection of canonical 19th century works, to the neglect of contemporary music and, by his reckoning, works that were too complex, peripheral or contrapuntal. All of Toscanini's efforts were now concentrated on mass appeal of a highly restricted type — "all-purpose performance excitement correlative with Verdian visceral mechanics." In Studio 8H at NBC — symbolic of the maestro's aloofness, his invisibility and inaccessibility, the quasi-scientific ballyhoo of the corporation's "merchandizing mindset" — Toscanini and the orchestra churned out their weekly "legendary" performances, performances whose shrunken content was embellished with the hype and worshipful commentary of a battery of corporate flunkies.

I thought I was learning. I was only being indoctrinated.

I know I learned that thousands died among the whites and more among the Indians in the great wagon train migrations from the Mississippi westward. I was probably wrong about that, too, even though the movies and the radio programs and the western novels and some serious western historians told me it was so. Then along came John D. Unruh's book, *The Plains Across*, which on the basis of painstaking research tells me, for example, that between 1840 and 1860 only about 350 emigrants and about 420 Indians were killed in encounters with each other. Most accounts of terrible depredations on the wagon trains were semifictional and based largely on rumors.

Did I learn any good lessons well? I don't know. I begin to doubt.

Try another lesson I thought I learned. I didn't really get to know motion pictures until 1939 and later. The world had discovered them somewhat sooner, but until that time my family had lived in a small rural town. There was a movie house there, but it wasn't always open in those depression days, and when it was open, my family didn't always have a dime to spare for a movie. Then we moved to the city, to a house scarcely two blocks away from a neighborhood movie house, where one could see three new movies a week and we could by then sometimes find the dimes. In the early years of World War II I saw *Captains of the Clouds*, *A Yank in the RAF*, *Fighter Squadron*, and God knows how many other movies featuring what we then referred to as "the gallant lads" of the Royal Air Force in their Spitfires and Hurricanes and Lancasters and Wellingtons and Beaufighters and Mosquitos. They were, I thought, surely the grandest creatures on earth. Then, not long ago, from a harrowing book by Martin Middlebrook called *The Battle of Hamburg*, I learned a little about versions of their deeds we were never told about during the war years. (Sometimes I think that everyone else has always known the truth about things, and I only later learn fragments of it all.) Early in the war, the RAF commenced building a large fleet of bombers for nighttime bombing. This fleet was not intended for precision bombing of military targets but for area bombing. Middlebrook reports that Sir Arthur Harris issued a directive in February 1942:

"The primary object of your operation should now be focused on the morale of the enemy civilian population." The bomber fleet was built and ready by summer 1943. A Bomber Command Operations order of May 27, 1943, called for "total destruction of the city of Hamburg." There followed, in the period from July 24 to August 3, four raids. On the second raid, conducted through the night of July 27–28, the planes carried an unusually high proportion of incendiary explosives. With the large quantity of incendiary bombs falling at a time of hot, dry weather, a fierce firestorm quickly developed. Later reports indicate temperatures in some sections of the city as high as eight hundred degrees. Forty thousand people died in Hamburg that night, incinerated if outside, asphyxiated, then burned, if inside. An eyewitness cited in Middlebrook's book tells of burned victims, still alive, stuck in the melted asphalt of the streets, screaming, their minds gone. I've had some difficulty fitting this new knowledge into the world I had created before. I was not alone in thinking of the men of the RAF as "gallant lads." That is how we came to know them then. We did not know them as fire bombers of civilians. They were not revealed to us in that way. Someone didn't tell us what there was to know. I learned some wrong lessons. And yet I cannot easily surrender what I first learned. Sylvia Moss's poem "Green Fields of France" tells of a man who went looking in the fields of France for the heroism he'd learned about, who

> stood
> helpless among the white crosses
> as if to say *I'm sorry.*
> *I missed the Great War.*
> *I was born in thirty-one,*
> *even too young for the second.*
>
> If he could,
> he'd apologize to every pilot
> who ever kept a journal.
>
> Yet what sends him hunting
> for Omaha Beach, wrecked Spitfires,

the first lines of the British,
is not pity, but the occasion for courage.
He would give up anything
to have this chance,
to spiral down from the sky, RAF-style,
still believing in the enemy.

What else did I learn? Strange things, powerful when I learned them, though wrong. I learned that "the angle of the dangle is directly proportional to the heat of the meat," and that

It's not the length, it's not the size—
It's how many times you can make it rise.

And it was a long time, maybe not until yesterday, before I learned that neither piece of wisdom has any relation to either physiological truth or sexual pleasure. The gap between the expectations of a predictable, probably WASPish, and maybe Baptist world and almost any reality is astonishing. I came to suppose that physiological truth probably had something to do with how many appendages and how many apertures or special places any set of bodies might have. As to sexual pleasure, I guess I had come at some time to suppose that it was known—truly known—only to a handful of libertines and wonderfully sophisticated rich folks. Otherwise, such pleasure, I had guessed, must be illicit. Imagine my surprise. Imagine my surprise when I learned the other day that even respectable folks love to fuck, and apparently do. Imagine my surprise when, for example, I stumbled on Robert Craft's essay "Amorous in Amherst," a review of Polly Longsworth's *Austin and Mabel: The Amherst Affair and Love Letters of Austin Dickinson and Mabel Loomis Todd*, and read that on December 13, 1883,

Austin Dickinson, fifty-four, married for twenty-six years and the father of three became the lover of Mabel Loomis Todd, thirty years younger, married for four years and the mother of Millicent. The consummation took place in Emily's and her sister Lavinia's dining room, in which Emily sometimes wrote. The diaries of Austin and Mabel reveal that their extramarital rites were repeated thereafter about twelve times a month, then somewhat less frequently from 1886 until Austin's death in 1895. The testimony of Maggie Maher, the sisters' housekeeper, in Lavinia's 1896 lawsuit against the Todds, places a higher estimate on the number of rendezvous and adds that they took place "sometimes in the afternoon and sometimes in the fore-noon. . . . Sometimes for three or four hours just as their consciences allowed them."

Longsworth bases Mabel's "energetic physical commitment" on evidence that on several of those days each month she was also entertaining her husband. And imagine my surprise when I read that in the autumn of 1885, when the Todds moved to a new house, Mabel and Austin made love on ten or more occasions, in the presence of a witness, as Austin recorded it, the witness apparently being Mabel's husband. What a strange world, and I learned nothing of it save wrong or peculiar lessons.

Item: I learned that my brothers and I and my male cousins and my uncles and my male kinfolk, related or not, all over the world had denied women their own character, had transformed them for the benefit of our own fantasies. How the hell was I to know, back then? How the hell was I to know that Andrea Dworkin would write: "Physically, the woman in intercourse is a space inhabited, a literal territory occupied literally: occupied even if there has been no resistance, no force; even if the occupied person said yes please, yes hurry, yes more. . . . Intercourse is the pure, sterile, formal expression of men's contempt for women." I was wrong to commence with, and now I'm apparently wrong again: I didn't know it was occupation; I thought it was homage, testimony, embrace. I tried to unlearn my wrong lessons, and they want to tell me that I am wrong again.

But it's been a long time now since I was surprised to be wrong. I look at the notes I kept over the years while I was trying to make a garden. I see the county extension horticulturist's advice about gardening schedules and methods. I compare that with the notes I kept of my own efforts. All I see of my own effort is, at the first, traces of good intentions, and then, as the sun grew hotter, some evidence that I was mostly intent on getting through and getting back into the air-conditioned house, though I was earnest about wanting lots of black-eyed peas. I believe I thought that sooner or later the dust storms would come anyway. They had come in the 1930s, and I had seen them. I could still smell them inside my head. They'd come again and forever. Of Dust Bowl times, Marilyn Coffey writes: "The storms were not perpetual, but they began to seem that way. 'There is rarely a day when at some time dust clouds do not roll over,' wrote Caroline Henderson, an Oklahoma farm woman, for the *Atlantic Monthly*. Oklahoma counted 102 storms in the span of one year; North Dakota reported 300 in eight months' time. Most arrived early in the day and lasted until nightfall, but some raged through the night, and a few blew for days." Some "they" taught us to work hard, to call no attention to ourselves, to stay clean, to work slowly upward toward security; but the evidence suggests that the dust storms will always blow, that the desert, some desert, will always win.

How do you remember guilt, disgrace, honorable victory, honorable defeat, and success if the way you first learned them was maybe altogether wrong, or maybe right but altogether mismatched to any world that any soul ever lived in? When persuasive people and daily evidence both testify otherwise, how do you continue to believe — and how wrong would you be if you did — that suffering is noble, that love is always accompanied by chivalric behavior, that the WASP family of 1934 is the appropriate goal of nostalgic dreaming, that true believers will at last be saved? In West Texas, A. C. Greene says,

> God doesn't like for His people to pick and pry, to seek beyond his Sacred Page, to say, aloud or in their hearts, "I wonder . . ." God chastises those who say they know too much, who taunt Him with their knowledge, who refuse to accept their lives as His will.
>
> Nothing can change that, for the sun is his eye, and it is so brassy it seems to be a mirror, following you with a blinding shaft no matter which way you turn. And a man is weak; he

feels and thinks inside things the sun would dry out and the wind blow away if they were exposed; therefore such thoughts are suspect.

Once in a while I paid attention, took notice, learned a small lesson that was right.

On Wednesday, September 26, 1973, I learned that when children grow up, they sometimes go out in the rain and get wet and sometimes you don't even know about it and so can't worry about it at the right time.

On Wednesday, May 15, 1974, I noticed that all of the people of the house were at home, that the house was still, and that they slept safely.

On Tuesday, May 17, 1988, I learned that while I wasn't watching, I had become old folks, part of the oldest generation.

Shit. I wasn't ready.

Even then, I learned that I was still wrong and still believed what was wrong. Still believed, despite family lessons. Uncle Bill was maybe seventy-five (but I'm not sure) when he died. Got along fine for a while there without some part of his stomach and gut, but then the cancer quit being patient and he died. My father would have known his age. Uncle Dee died on July 2, 1988. He was maybe eighty (but I'm not sure), played tennis until last year. My father would have known his age. I didn't ask. I didn't ask their age, didn't ask him all the questions I had meant to ask. Maybe the time was wrong. Or maybe I forgot. He didn't wait. He died in May at eighty-two.

Maybe evidence doesn't count.

When you learn strong lessons early, however wrong, no evidence seems to count against them. Uncle Bill was about seventy-five. Uncle Dee was about eighty. My father was eighty-two. Grandpa Durham was on past eighty. Grandma Durham was on past seventy, and so was Grandma Corder.

But in May 1988, the main thing I was trying to do was to live to be fifty-nine. Evidence doesn't matter. Maybe it's the first death that matters. Grandpa Corder died in 1938 at age fifty-eight. He was in the casket in our house, brought there from Robinson's Grocery and Hardware with mortuary in the rear ("All Your Needs from the Cradle to the Grave"), and I thought you were supposed to die at fifty-eight. Evidence doesn't count. All the rest are alive except Aunt Nell. But you're supposed to die at fifty-eight. The other day, in September 1988, I made it to fifty-nine, and I still don't believe the evidence. What I learned was wrong, but I still believe. Evidence, you know, has to match belief, or it's not evidence.

But once in a while I paid attention, took notice, learned a small lesson that was right.

I learned to be melancholy. I don't know that anyone taught me. I breathe the bracing air of expected grief.

I learned that pretty well, and it's more than likely a right lesson.

Most things I learned didn't turn out to be right, or if they were right, I forgot. Joseph Colin Murphy's poem "Panhandle Piety" has a speaker who testifies to his heritage:

> My father
> taught me
> not to cry
> not to lie
> or cheat
>
> and not
> to die
> easy
>
> To beat
> the best
> and to eat
> what was bless'd
> and set
> before me

I have cried. I have lied. I have cheated. I'll die, however. I haven't beat the best. I have refused food that was blessed.

I have not learned how to be sure, how to be brave. I studied with the Scarlet Pimpernel to learn how to be a hero, and I didn't make it. I pored over the scripture I found in *Beau Geste*. Later, I was struck to find that hosts of humankind had not received the vision. The Geste brothers told what brothering should be, I thought; they defined family, I thought, and gallantry.

Later, with a somewhat larger cast of characters, I forgot to keep the covenant. I didn't make it as far as gallantry. Still, it was the way I thought living might be, while I waited to be good Digby, old Dig. But then we had no John to come back and tell our story, and my brother didn't know that he was Beau, and after a while I forgot to be Digby.

YONDER

27

Jackleg Carpentry

When I was young, I'd watch the grown folks at hard times—maybe, say, when Grandpa Corder died in 1938—and they'd talk quietly, working out the solemn things that waited to be done, and I remember wondering when you learned how to do such things as waited to be done.

On Tuesday, May 17, 1988, we told the man we wanted the blue casket with light blue lining, not the bronze with beige lining. I had turned around scarcely twice, and I found myself alongside my sister, beside my brother, talking quietly, working out the solemn things that waited to be done. I remembered that no one had taught us how. I wondered whether or not—despite the managerial expertise we seem to treasure now, despite flow charts and systems, despite prioritized philosophies and master plans, despite cost accounting, despite bottom lining—we mostly do jackleg work, waiting until we learn, working until we learn, but no one teaches us.

I came into the twentieth century, through a sizable part of it, and on toward the later part of my life altogether unprepared. Many of the lessons I learned, maybe most of them, maybe all of them, were wrong. If I learned good lessons, I usually forgot. I came into the twentieth century not knowing how to do much. Being in the twentieth century has taught me little more. I keep trying to hold on to the world, to make a world, when no one taught me how, or if someone did, I didn't learn. I should have listened. I should have paid attention. I should have noticed. All I know how to do is make do, and that not well.

Not long ago, a colleague told me a little about an essay he had just finished. Since I have known him for some time, I expected that it would be well written, that he would have worked it meticulously. Apparently it came out just about right, for he was willing to be a little proud of it. I believe he felt that this time the work had turned out the way he wanted it to—he allowed as how he thought it was well crafted. That's the phrase he used. I haven't read it, but I expect it is.

I suppose all of us admire and cherish well-crafted things. Surprise and pleasure in what is made beautifully—a novel, a poem, a table, a chair, a garden, a song, a watch, a piece of molding, dilled green beans, biscuits—account in large part for the energy that drives us into and through our lives. I think I have prized well-crafted things. I remember a table my father made, and John Graves's book *Goodbye to a River*. I remember a certain cheesecake, and a no-hit game my son pitched when he was fifteen. I remember my older daughter's music, and my younger daughter's Christmas presents. I remember a particular fish dish. We look for the well crafted. We want, perhaps need, things to be well made, to stay fixed, to be eternal; we want, perhaps need, a post to hitch ourselves to so that we won't get loose. But we're always loose.

We're always doing jackleg work, trying to get things, and ourselves, fixed. Mostly that's all right: everything changes, nobody notifies us ahead of time, and we have to keep doing solemn things that nobody taught us how to do. Jackleg carpentry—and one can practice anything in the jackleg way—may be defined as that mode in which, upon completion of a job, the carpenter backs off, surveys the work, and says, "Well, there it is, by God—it ain't much, but it'll hold us until we can think of something better." I have often lamented jackleggery, including especially my own, have done my share of fussing about things that don't stay fixed, have sometimes longed for the sure principle that endures, the sure craft that makes things so they stay fixed, the well-built house that will still be there so that you can see it when you go back.

But that mostly isn't our way. We're mostly jackleg carpenters. Things change. People die. Places vanish. Memory fails. We've reason for woe. We look, but can't find the world that was, or ourselves in it. We're always having to do solemn things that nobody taught us how to do. That's mostly all right. Nothing is ever finished, over, done with, unless we decide so, and then we've already gone over to dogma. *Paradise Lost* still comes toward us unfinished, waiting for a reading. Samuel Johnson is oftener exploring than proclaiming, still trying to do the work that will let him be convinced that he has done the work—he still writes "I have done nothing" in his last prayers and meditations.

I know that when we decide something is fixed, right, over, we've accepted authority, elected tyranny, and elevated dogma. Freedom, I expect, lies the other way, in the provisional world of jackleg carpentry. We don't achieve freedom, of course; we are always unreleased, caught in nostalgia and loss in the long later time after great change, pulled one way and another in the conflict of rhetorics, always failing or about to fail, always on the point of disappearing. We don't achieve freedom; we are always in some world, thinking the thoughts that can be thought there, doing the work that can be done there, hunting for a way—a jackleg way—to build a new scaffold, a new world to stand on. We improvise. We try again. We're always provisional.

I know that's all right. But it's sure as hell scary.

28

Domestic Privacies

If I'll just pay attention, I often think, if I'll just give due notice, I often think, if I'll really mark the day, I often think, then I can hold people and places and events and things in my mind and always carry them with me. But, of course, I didn't always listen and watch, didn't always pay attention, didn't always take notice, didn't always mark the days that should have been marked, and all of them should have been marked. And when I did listen and watch, pay attention, take notice, and mark the days, I only heard and saw and attended and noticed and marked in my way, and that was insufficient and maybe wrong. No one can set the record straight. What I heard and saw and attended and noticed and marked, insufficiently and probably in error, I then, no doubt, misremembered. The past is not impervious to change. In the fall, everything changes, and memory fails.

So it is, I think, with most of us, but probably not with all of us—maybe even all of us, though I hope not. In some, I hope, an intensity of attention overcomes oblivion. In a review of Chaim Grade's *My Mother's Sabbath Days*, Herbert Gold remarks that "in 'My Mother's Sabbath Days'—a long and dense chronicle written after World War II, in which he describes his own survival, or *partial* survival, of the Holocaust—Grade means to cheat the angel of death with more than sentimental evocation of his destroyed universe. His memory grows dense and muscular because history demands it of him." I haven't read *My Mother's Sabbath Days*. I hope he made it. I hope he cheated the angel of death and forgetfulness. I don't know what history is but what we remember, and mostly we remember in error.

But I think memory holds a little better and error diminishes a little as we save the blessed particulars of our lives. "I'm all for anything," Jay Parini writes, "that makes you feel / the gravity afoot, the tug of light / particulars." If any kind of truth is going to come to be kept, it will be found saved, Mark Doty says, in concrete and blessed particulars, where "detail redeems memory." Observation and rendition of particulars will not necessarily yield or keep truth. One moment isn't all of time, or one look a whole view, or one sense of things a revelation about all things. And besides, I might forget and tell the particular so that another would not know it. To demand our particular experience of another is arrogance and dogma, but to offer our particular experience to another is about the only plenitude we can hope to achieve, and may even be enough. Dr. Johnson praised biography because the biographer can take us to the lives of particular persons "not distinguished by any striking or wonderful vicissitudes." The biographer, he reckoned, can "lead the thoughts into domestic privacies, and display the minute details of daily life," reminding us that "there are many invisible circumstances which . . . are more important than public occurrences." Often, though, we don't seem to have a memory for the particular, or we don't know that we have a memory for the particular, or we don't know that our memory counts for others. We only announce ourselves in the direction of each other, declare our definitions at each other, speak as authorities before each other, though we may want to know ourselves and to show ourselves to each other. Paying attention to domestic privacies might let us sometimes see and know the people, the places, the events, the things among which we frail humans reside and have our hopes and woes, might let us hold in our minds what Dr. Johnson called the incidents "of a volatile and evanescent kind, such as soon escape the memory, and are rarely transmitted by tradition." In Francine Prose's novel *Household Saints*, this passage appears: "Maybe the burning bush was burning all the time and Moses didn't notice. Maybe the miracle is when you stop and pay attention." The one rock we try to dig up, Miller Williams says, "may have been buried where it was / to hold the county in place." Then what do we do, Williams asks, if madness, old age, and death come close?

We take our breaths and loves to let them go
and tell the names of things to the forgetful air.

29

Long Walks

And maybe get everything all wrong.

I can't get or set the record straight.

We took long walks together.

I guess we don't know the same long walks. A blessed particular to one may look like something else or nothing to another.

We took long walks together. All the way to Rotterdam and down the Rhine to Mannheim. Wasn't that a time?

From poor up to adequate. Wasn't that a time?

That time in New York: we set out northward from the hotel, thinking to look and to see our way up to Central Park, and wound up walking through the park in the nose-running cold all the way to the Metropolitan Museum. Wasn't that a time?

And that time in the mountains? We went to the Indian Lodge in the Davis Mountains State Park, where a mountain on either side filled our eyes, and we climbed them both the long way, and we found the place where the deer slept. Wasn't that a time?

And we walked separately to Henderson Street, to the lawyer's office. That was a time.

But damn my soul, Babe, if I can keep the time straight, or the route we took every time.

Was it in the summer of 1982, that time we went to Washington when we still had the little Chevrolet that we liked? The summer before I spent the spring term in the hospital? When we went to see Cathy? When we put the back seat down and made a little pallet down one side so that either of us could rest while the other was driving? You fit better than I did.

We drove up the southerly way, I remember, through Dallas to Shreveport and on through Vicksburg and Jackson and Meridian and Tuscaloosa and up to Birmingham. Then we slanted up to Chattanooga and drove up to Lookout Mountain. From there, I'm not sure. I think we drove a little way to the northeast on Interstate 75, then drove through wonderful backcountry—I think first on Highway 64, then Highway 411, then Highway 321—to Gatlinburg, but we didn't stop there. The place was crowded with tourists. Instead, we drove on to where the Blue Ridge Parkway begins and drove along to somewhere in the vicinity of Boone, North Carolina, maybe actually in Boone, where we spent the night.

We had decided that we'd be too much delayed in reaching Washington if we stayed on the parkway. The next morning we headed north—I'm not sure just how, maybe it was on Highway 221, then Highway 21, and got on Interstate 81 for Washington. I'm not sure.

But it's the return trip I'm thinking about. As I recall it, I think I got it in my mind that we should see some new country on the way back, and I think we went out from Washington and on down through West Virginia to Charleston and Huntington, then on to Lexington, across Kentucky, down to Memphis, and home. It's the first stretch I can't get straight, and I wish I could because of what I saw there.

Maybe it was Highway 50 we took, westerly out of Washington. If that was the road, then we went across a piece of Virginia, a first little stretch of West Virginia, a tiny corner of Maryland, then on down again in West Virginia. If that is the way it was, then what I'm remembering was probably in that first stretch of West Virginia, as we were crossing the Allegheny Mountains.

I guess it wasn't much, but it has stayed in my mind. I was driving and you were napping in the back. The road became wonderfully crooked, the hills rougher, the valleys deeper and darker. Then I came up a rise, as I remember, and rounded a curve, and there it was, all down before me: a sudden drop down a series of sharp switchbacks—what was it, three, four, maybe five hairpins down the mountain into the deep green valley, cabins nearly out of sight in the blue shadows? I wish to God I had waked you up that time, Babe, so you could have seen it.

30

Hiding

I can't get time fixed, can't get or set the record straight. I hid from my daughter. On a Sunday, January 25, 1987. It wasn't a game, for I wasn't playing, and I am old and she is grown and might not like my game were it a game, hid from her on a Sunday.

I had worked all morning in my office. At noon I went to get the Sunday *New York Times* at the Century Book Store, as I do just about every Sunday. Perhaps I was five or ten minutes later than usual. Perhaps that's why it happened. I left the building where my office is, angled across University Drive, along the front and around the end of the science building, headed east on Bowie Street, crossed into the big parking lot and on to the alley that runs beside the office supply store behind the bookstore. I had gone around the office supply store and had started around the corner of the bookstore when I saw her. She had, I think, just come out of the bookstore—she likes the Sunday *Times* too—and was getting into her car. I stepped quickly behind the corner of the building. Perhaps she saw me. Perhaps she didn't. I hid, at any rate. I hid.

I could, I guess, tell some of my reasons for hiding. Perhaps I know most or all of my reasons and might say—but not yet, if ever, if I know. I'll think about that later. For now, it's enough to think about being stunned by my own behavior: I hid. How often, Daughter, have I gone to seek, not to hide? What I have done before doesn't justify me, Daughter, but how often have I gone to see, to be seen, not to hide? I don't want to try to justify myself, Daughter. I won't be justified. I want only to remember and to puzzle and to tug at this: I wanted to see you, wanted always to be where I could be seen, but I hid. I hid.

I didn't hide before, or so I thought, wanted always to be in plain sight. I remember picking you up when school was out at Paschal High School, remember wanting to be plain to you in the crowd along Forest Park Boulevard. I remember being late and frantic to pick you and Mindy up at the Scott Theater. You'd been to see *High Noon*, but it was dark and I wasn't there in plain sight. At Mo Ranch that time, I wanted you to know we were there. I wanted to be sure to park where you could see me when I came to pick you up at church after Senior High Fellowship, wanted you to find me, wanted to find you.

I have been grateful ever since for a moment when we saw each other – I think it was in your freshman year at TCU, and you were living in the dormitory, and it was a Saturday, I know. Some books were due at the public library, and it seemed a time for browsing. I called you to see if you wanted to go, too. You thought not, this time. I fiddled around for a while, getting myself together, got in the car, turned around in the driveway, pulled out onto Devitt – and there you were, there you were, just rounding the corner off Odessa Street. You'd changed your mind. I've been grateful ever since: another moment and I'd have missed you; another moment and I'd have been gone; another moment and we'd not have seen each other.

I always wanted you to find me, but always as much, or more, to see you as to be seen, to know where you are, were, will be.

I've studied my map of Washington, trying to get you located. I'm pretty sure about the Jefferson Memorial, Daughter, and have never been so moved by any other public monument: "I have sworn upon the altar of Almighty God eternal vigilance against any form of tyranny over the minds of men." I should have paid closer attention to that, Daughter, shouldn't I? And your apartment that first time? Not far east of the Capitol? Do I have it right? Your office that time, at the National Association for the Education of Young Children, was not far off the White House to the northwest, at 1834 Connecticut Avenue, N.W., and Vincenzo was nearby, at 1606 Twentieth Street, N.W. But where was the wonderful Ethiopian restaurant you took us to, Daughter, and what was it called, and how shall I ever find you there?

And where do you live now? And where is your office?

I wanted to be in plain sight, to be there; but as much, I wanted to see you, as you were, are, will be.

Last fall, in October, I went to Chicago, Daughter, to see my publisher. I'd been, I know, increasingly difficult for them to work with, and we needed to visit. My appointment was on Wednesday morning. I flew in at about noon on Tuesday and rented a car. I checked in at the hotel where the publisher had reserved a room, the North Shore Hilton, then toodled around a while and visited a pipe store on Dempster.

Then I went to Evanston, Daughter, and tried to find you, but you weren't there. I parked near the Holiday Inn and walked and looked. I found Fritz That's It, and it looked much as I remembered, but I couldn't find the museum shop where you volunteered on Saturdays. Then I walked south on Chicago Street, turned west on Washington at the newsstand, then south again on Custer, and there was the building where your apartment was.

You weren't there. When you were there—this Sunday—I hid so you wouldn't see me.

I had always wanted to be there, locatable, if you or David or Mindy needed me; had hated, feared, not being there, wherever there was, and wanted to know how and where you all were at every moment. Perhaps I wanted sameness and sureness as sanity, Cathy. Do you know what August 1977 was like for me? Why should you? I don't know what August 1977 was like for you, and love you altogether without knowing about that August. But do you know about August? Knowing your mind, I'd guess you probably know better than I: in the first week David was married, and left; in the third week you helped your mother and me move Mindy to the dormitory at SMU for her freshman year, and she left; then we loaded you into the rented van, and you and your mother set off for Evanston, and I was alone. Perhaps I wanted sameness, sureness, perpetuity as sanity.

If that is so, then it was I who ruptured any sameness, sureness, perpetuity, sanity, and now I hide.

Do you know why? Do I know why? I try to guess it out.

I hid because I was ashamed, ashamed that I had betrayed and abandoned all of you, had—I must accept the appearance, the function of my acts—repudiated you, hid because I thought you wouldn't want to see me.

I hid because I was still imagining myself to be important enough to disturb you. I am a disturbance, a violation of the order of things, and I didn't want to disturb you, to discompose any sameness, sureness, perpetuity, saneness, or whatever you might have composed for yourself. Some of what I composed, or thought I composed, for myself had cracks and holes in it.

Oh, Cathy, I thought all along that I was gentle and undemanding. In other eyes I was insistent, domineering, always wanting to define the world in my way, to claim it for myself, to hold it. I didn't compose well, and I misread my own text.

Interesting, isn't it, Cathy, how wrong we sometimes take the world, how we create it, or re-create it, to our need and convenience? A few months ago, on a trip to Jayton, I finally found copies of the *Jayton Chronicle* that I'd been looking for, issues from 1934 to 1945. How I came to find them is another story. What's astonishing is how wrong I was, how erroneously, how mischievously, I created the world I thought I remembered. I read the paper, now microfilmed, and learn that much was otherwise than I had thought or known. Uncle Nolan wasn't the first-string guard on Jayton's first football team in 1938; he was a substitute, though he played a lot in place of Jiggs Holley; and besides, it wasn't the school's first football team — there had been a team back in the 1920s. I didn't even have the name of the movie theater right: it was first the Palace, then the Kent, then the Avalon, then the Texan, but never the Texas. I was wrong about the undertaker, too. I thought undertaking, such as it might have been, was undertaken at the back of Jones's Drug, on the north side of the square. It wasn't. All along it was done in back of Robinson's Grocery and Hardware ("All Your Needs from the Cradle to the Grave," the advertisement says in the *Chronicle*), on the east of the square. That was Mr. Charles Robinson. His brother, Baker, worked with him and was the father of Peggy Sue Robinson, whom I loved deeply from afar until the fourth grade. I had a lot wrong. Along the way, for example, there was a café called the "Green Castle" somewhere opposite Huls Drug Store and the movie theater, and I'd have sworn there were no buildings there at all.

And why didn't I know, Cathy, what the time was like, why

didn't I know about the ruins, deep in the distant county south and west of Jayton, somewhere in the ravines along the Double Mountain Fork of the Brazos, ruins of an Anglo or European settlement, not ancient but predating the better-known white settlers of the county? They were hidden from me all this time, and I hid them from myself by not studying enough to know they were there. I wanted to find them. They were hidden, and I hid. They weren't lost; it's only that I was lost to them. I wanted to find you, to be found. I am not lost. I am not lost, not lost.

31

To the Jayton Cemetery

But what lessons did I learn at your knee, dear Mother, or miss, or mislearn, or misremember? I can't let go: What lessons? And why do I ask only you, who cannot hear me now? You weren't my only instructor. I might have learned lessons good and bad and misremembered all from my father. Or from the preacher down at the Baptist church, or from Mr. Holley, the only Sunday school teacher I can remember. Or from Jimmy Mathews or Don Jones or Bobby Sproules, though it's unlikely they'd have sermonized, except unaware. Or from Mamie Morris Murphy Fowler, my first-grade teacher, or from Nannie Beth Rice, my second-grade teacher, or from Sue Kinney, my third-grade teacher, whom I loved deeply and not too wildly from afar, or from Mrs. Check Jay, my fourth-grade teacher, but not from Mrs. Bradley, my fifth-grade teacher. Or I might have learned, and did, from Grandma and Grandpa Durham, but less from Grandma and Grandpa Corder. Or I might have learned, and did, from Aunt Cora or Aunt Nell or especially my brother, or from the air in Jayton or from the gyp water we sometimes drank. Or from God come down hard off the Caprock in a blowing dust storm, bouncing and throwing tumbleweeds along a lonesome field to hang against a far and lonesome fence, or maybe shouting to me out of the whirlwind that twists up along the canyon's rim, washing me less than clean at last, baptized in the muddy water of Credit Lake. Why ask you alone, dear Mother, who can no longer hear me? It might have been the year or day or drought that lessoned me, or John Calvin, waiting in the far blue of Putoff Canyon.

And if I learned some lessons, what lessons did I miss, dear Mother, miss, forget, or remember but misunderstand?

Why did you deprive me of Heaven, dear Mother, you and all those others? Why did you and all those others — and I, oh yes and only—make a Heaven in my mind I cannot reach, a Hell I cannot miss?

You forswore your lessons, changed beyond them, and maybe never knew you taught what I missed, forgot, or misunderstood, or maybe never taught, however much I learned.

I remember what you taught me about the hymn, when I found myself half humming, half singing that song from old times. It had a hole in it, a single word that I couldn't get in memory. The hymn was "On Jordan's Stormy Banks," and I couldn't remember a word in the fourth line of the first verse. From the rhythm, I was pretty sure it was a four-syllable word. I called and asked if you could provide the word. "What goes in the blank space?" I asked, and sang:

> On Jordan's stormy banks I stand
> And cast a wistful eye,
> Where Canaan's fair and happy land,
> And my HUM HUM HUM HUM lie.

You were quiet, and then I heard you singing and humming:

> On Jordan's HUM HUM banks I HUM
> And cast a HUM HUM eye,
> Where Canaan's HUM and happy land
> And my—

"It's *possessions*," you said

> Where Canaan's fair and happy land,
> And my possessions lie.

And I understood why I thought it was four syllables; you sang "po-o-ses-sions." Okay, I thought. It's "possessions." But then it came to me that this didn't sound right. You were still on the telephone. "But if they're across the river and you've never been there," I asked, "how can they be your *possessions*?" Nothing for a moment. Then you said, very patiently, "Well, according to the doctrine of grace, what lies there waiting *is* yours, even if you haven't been there before. Didn't you pay any attention in church?" "Oh," I said, "I see." How strange this was, I remember thinking. You didn't talk that way in old times. Had you the audacity to have grown and learned and changed during all the time I thought I had you fixed in my mind? I guess you did. I guess you decided that you were real apart from my interpretation of you. You didn't notify me to change, though, but I was changing all along.

After the divorce I was a different text. Or perhaps a continuing text, but not the text that some claim in memory, for memory is always wrong. What she knows is not what I know. What I was is not what I am. What I am is not what I was. What I was is not what I was. What I am is not what I am. What I am is not here, but waits on another's reading, maybe here, maybe there. I can't testify to my own existence. Won't. Don't know how. Might. Better not. Can't.

Notes for these few paragraphs occur on Saturday, May 16, 1987. How strange life is. Severance occurs and does not occur. I am cut off and I am not cut off. What was is and will be. What will be is and was. "Lord, why am I thinking about this?" David Bottoms writes, and then,

> Lord, is it possible
> to fall toward grace? Could I be moved
> to believe in new beginnings? Could I be moved?

How do I testify to griefs and horrors in my mind — but not to all, no, not to all? I still have that old need to mark the day, to save it. And where — and why — did that need rise? Will I ever know? Will I ever explain myself? Will I ever see myself except as my own interpretation of myself?

Perhaps it doesn't matter where or how I grew up. Perhaps what matters, what I cannot change, is how I thought I grew up. Rilke remarked somewhere, "Don't think life is more than what's packed into childhood." Another would describe it differently, would see it differently. We don't always see what we see. I begin at last, though not entirely, to understand why the Double Mountains are always blue and why they loom so large from almost anywhere you look in Kent County or Stonewall County. They're always blue, a startling and mysterious blue, until you get within two or three miles of the lower slopes. I thought blue was a condition of existence, and I guess it is: my friend tells me that what lies between the Double Mountains and me—and, oh, so much lies between me and the Double Mountains—refracts light and air and time and turns the mountains blue.

But I hadn't begun until yesterday to understand—and still don't, not entirely—why they seem so high, so big, there on the horizon of my life. On my desk I have a photograph of the Double Mountains and a sketch, both made at the same place, the Brazos bridge. In the sketch the mountains dominate the scene. In the photograph they're blue, yes, but low and unprepossessing. The photograph image, another friend tells me, is pretty much like the image on my retina; but then my retina lies to my brain, or brain doesn't want to hear the story retina tells. They look larger in the sketch, apparently, because, looking without the camera, we take distance cues into account and maintain some size constancy inside our heads. In my head I know they're larger than everything, so no matter where I see them from, I keep their hugeness constant. The camera does not take notice of distance cues. The photographer who wants to show how we perceive a full moon will have to use a telephoto lens, or else the moon will look much smaller than we think we perceive it. I saw them, my retina caught an image of them, but I changed their size inside my head. I don't know what looking tells you, but looking from the Brazos bridge is good.

I grew up, so it seemed to me, in troubled circumstances, in a life I thought was woe, waiting for blessed hereafter but always expecting grief, learning harder lessons than anyone ever taught me, whether at home or down at the Baptist church or wherever, was always, I sometimes think—no, always think—expecting grief, not knowing if it would be deprivation, loss, sorrow, damnation, not knowing which might be worse.

I changed, of course, but never lost my expectation, and do not know where I learned to wait for grief.

If I learned some lessons, what lessons did I miss, Preacher, miss, forget, or remember but misunderstand?

Why did you deprive me of Heaven, Preacher, you and all

those others? Why did you and all those others—and I, oh yes and only—make a Heaven in my mind I cannot reach, a Hell I cannot miss?

I changed, but kept my sacred lessons, though I've never known exactly what they are, and kept them only in my mind, not in my behavior:

1. Stay clean. Don't be like poor white trash.
2. Don't make scenes. Don't call attention to yourself.
3. Be pure or go to Hell.
4. Be faithful somehow to something or you'll lose everything.

Where did I learn such lessons, and why? Oh, dear Mother, Father, Preacher, Brother, what lessons did I miss, forget, or remember but misunderstand? Why did you deprive me of Heaven, Mother, Father, Preacher, Brother? Why did you and all those others—and I, oh yes and only—make a Heaven in my mind I cannot reach, a Hell I cannot miss?

How did all of you learn to be sure? To trust your own memory? To know that you had identity. How did you learn to tell such awful truths that became to me not lies but truths I cannot approach, know, enter, understand? "When we all get together," one hymn says,

> What a day of rejoicing that will be!
> When we all see Jesus,
> We'll sing and shout the Jubilee?

And who is it, tell me, Mother, Father, Preacher, Brother, that I'll join? With whom will I gather to sing and shout the Jubilee? "Stand up, stand up, for Jesus!" another says,

> The strife will not be long:
> This day the noise of battle;
> The next the victor's song.
> To him that overcometh,
> A crown of life shall be;
> He with the King of glory
> Shall reign eternally.

Where, tell me, Mother, Father, Preacher, Brother, Sister; and whose company shall I keep, and what age will each of you choose to be? You tell me my questions will vanish:

> When I tread the verge of Jordan,
> Bid my anxious fears subside;
> Death of death, and hell's destruction,
> Land me safe on Canaan's side.

Have I vanished, Mother, Father, Preacher, Brother, do my friends despise, forsake me?

> Take it to the Lord in prayer;
> In his arms he'll take and shield thee,
> Thou wilt find a solace there.

But I have not, have only glimpsed a Heaven I cannot reach, a Hell I cannot miss, though some singer in my mind tells that "the Lord brings back his own," tells that "Jesus is merciful, Jesus will save," tells that

> There is a fountain filled with blood,
> Drawn from Immanuel's veins;
> And sinners, plunged beneath that flood,
> Lose all their guilty stains.

> The dying thief rejoiced to see
> That fountain in his day;
> And there may I, though vile as he,
> Wash all my sins away.

Others seem to know; seem to know their own identity, seem to know that their memories have rendered all things faithfully, seem to have a sure account of the world and hereafter. Perhaps they don't: perhaps they're only murmuring charms against death, against oblivion, against insignificance. Nevertheless, when I'm alone in the dark, they seem sure.

I wander through the cemetery in Jayton and find evidences of faith, or charms against death. I find the Smith family plot. Louis C. Smith died on April 18, 1976, for one reason or another unable to linger after Leona T. Smith died on April 15, 1976. Below their names, this appears: "Forever together in God's kingdom." Farther, I find the Rice family plot with George Rice, dead in 1933, and Lula Knudson Rice, dead in 1962. My second-grade teacher is there, too. She's buried as Nannie Beth Brown, dead in 1950 at age forty-three. Why did you do that, Nannie Beth, why die so young, and I never knew you? Near her is her older sister, Callie Janet Rice, 1904–1917. I find a stone for Jimmy's father, James E. Matthews, born March 5, 1907, died April 5, 1940. I find a stone for H. J. Whatley, Jr., born April 11, 1920, died in the war, August 7, 1943. The Rice stones and the Matthews stone and the Whatley stone offer no testimony to sure companionship hereafter, but others do. Myrta Jean Browning O'Fallon was born on April 7, 1925, and died at twenty on May 14, 1945. The stone says, "In heaven there is one angel more." A small stone for a baby who lived scarcely over a month in 1912 says, "Weep not mother and father for me for I am waiting in glory for thee." Another stone, commemorating a death on August 7, 1913, says "One less to love on earth / one more to meet in heaven." Another says

> There's a beautiful region above the skies
> And I long to reach its shore
> For I know I shall find my treasure there
> The loved one gone before.

A stone dated October 23, 1916, tells this:

> Our darling one
> Has gone before
> To greet us on
> The blissful shore.

Noah Brannen lived from 1856 to 1912. Wife Ella lived from 1855 to 1930. Their stone says, "We will meet again."

And whom will I meet again? On what blissful shore to find which treasure? With whom be together forever when I am landed safe on Canaan's shore?

No matter. I won't land there, find a solace there. "Nellie Gray" is not sung for me:

Oh my darling Nellie Gray,
Up in Heaven there they say
They'll never take you from me anymore.

I know there are other ways to take life. I know that life invites
us to be open to a creation filled with copious wonders, trivialities, sorrows, and amazements, and even miracles, that to do or
say anything at all requires us to close. I know that others take
that as hope, as I have on occasion, and live gladly. Perhaps. No
matter. Where shall I stand if I'm to be open, or to close? "Come
home," the old hymn says, "come home / Ye who are weary come
home." I can't find it, though I wait and watch and listen while

They tell me of a home far beyond the skies,
O they tell me of a home far away.
O they tell me of a home where no storm clouds rise,
O they tell me of the unclouded day.

The skies I remember, the skies I think about, are dark skies,
full of the dust beating down off the Caprock. Life will go on,
but I'll be lost in dust and time and never find my place, or have
one. I am the grief that I was expecting, and a lonesome grave's
more fit than home for me. At my door, the song says, the leaves
are falling; a cold hard wind has come, and Willie Nelson doesn't
sing for me:

Some day when we meet up yonder,
We'll walk hand in hand again.

There is no someday. I don't know which we it would be. I can't
guess where yonder is. I won't find it.

32

Gateway

The end was before the beginning. The beginning was after the
end. Who knows at the time what a beginning is, what an end
might be? Life is a narrative we make, and not, with beginnings
and endings that only occur in our little fictions. I don't know the
Sun Dance, have not been with Ishatai on the Red River, can seldom nerve myself. I always thought I'd do things when I got big.
I got big a long time ago and didn't notice, never got my belly
button lined up with middle C.

I went to San Angelo on Saturday, April 25, 1987. I left at 6:30.
The day was bright. I went to see Mindy, my younger daughter,
and Bin, her husband, and Andrew, their son.

I went out through Cresson into Hood County. The county was
named for General John Bell Hood, famous with his Texas Brigade but later not so successful. I crossed the bulge in the Brazos
they call Lake Granbury, curving around the edge of the little
town on my right. Hiram Granbury had been a lawyer in Texas
before he went off to war; he came to lead his own Texas Brigade
and was killed in battle in Tennessee in November 1864. Not far
to the north, in 1855, Mr. Pleasant Thorp settled near a mineral
spring. Later, the Clark brothers came down from Fort Worth
and founded the college that eventually became Texas Christian
University. Thorp Spring had a little moment as a health resort
and was a stop on the line from Fort Worth to Yuma, Arizona,
once the longest continuous stage line in the country, though for a
good part of the way folks rode in a buck wagon, not a stagecoach.

I went on through Tolar and Bluffdale, crossed the South Paluxy,
went into Erath County, and stopped at Stephenville for breakfast. Empty Thurber lies to the north, its coal mines long since
vacant, almost all of its buildings razed. John Stephen and others
settled in the area in 1855. Later, the county was named for George
Erath, who'd been born in Austria but came to Texas, fought at

San Jacinto, and served in the Congress of the Republic, then in the state legislature.

Out of Stephenville I drove on through Dublin, past the sign for Sardis Cemetery, into Comanche County, and through the little town of Comanche. Anglo settlers came into the area in 1854, but The People gave county and town their names. From Comanche I drove across Indian Creek and past the signs for Moro Cemetery, Eureka Cemetery, and Jenkins Springs Cemetery and alongside Pecan Bayou and into Brownwood. The town and Brown County were named for Henry S. Brown. Born in Kentucky, he came to Texas (but never to this area) and acquired considerable fame as an Indian fighter from 1825 to 1832, but he died in 1834. The Thirty-sixth Infantry Division of the Texas National Guard trained at Camp Bowie outside Brownwood; other units came later through World War II, but the camp is gone.

At the far edge of Brownwood I went up the sharp rise to higher ground, over Clear Water Creek, through Bangs, past Muke-water Cemetery and Salem Cemetery, and somewhere along there entered Coleman County. John Chisum built a store and saloon somewhere in the southeast part of the county in 1856, and in 1857 the army established Camp Colorado in the northeast. The county was named for Robert M. Coleman, who signed the Texas Declaration of Independence and was with Sam Houston at San Jacinto.

Long before I came to Santa Anna I could see the butte called Santa Anna Peak. The little town is built around its south base. Just at the far edge of Santa Anna, below the butte, the highway forks. The right-hand road goes to Coleman and Abilene. The left-hand road curves sharply west, goes over a bridge past the railroad tracks below, then rises to and through a deep cut in a rocky ridge.

That, Mindy says, is the gate to home. When she's been away, she says, and is driving back and comes to the fork in the road, the bridge, the rise, the deep-cut ridge, she knows she's home, has come to West Texas.

Just over the bridge I pulled over to stretch my legs and have a cup of coffee from the thermos and to look at Mindy's gateway.

Then I drove on, past Wild Cat Creek and Mustang Branch and through the little town of Valera, past Home Creek and through Talpa, past Mustang Creek and Middle Mustang and Mustang Creek again, past Butternut Creek and Bear Foot Creek and Long Branch and into Ballinger and over the Colorado River. Ballinger is the county seat of Runnels County, but it wasn't always.

A Spanish mission, called Mission San Clemente, was established in Runnels County in 1684, but Apaches ran the missionaries off. Nothing remains, and the site is uncertain, though there is a historical marker about twenty miles southeast of Bollinger. Anglo settlers didn't come until the early 1860s, and when the county was organized in 1880, it and its seat, Runnels City, took their name from Hiram G. Runnels, who'd been governor of Mississippi before he came to Texas in 1842. He was a delegate to the convention in 1845 that ratified annexation, and he wrote the new state's constitution. By 1885 Runnels City was hoping for a railroad, but a railroad agent paid for land on the Colorado River, and the rail line went there, to what is now Ballinger. For a big land sale on June 29, 1886, the railroad sent excursion trains, and the city was well under way. In 1887 the county seat was moved there.

After Ballinger, I drove on through Rowena, over Little Concho Creek, through Miles, past Mullins Cemetery, over Willow Creek and Crownest Creek and Valentine Branch, past the sign that said "Tennyson 22," over Red Creek, past the sign that said "Bronte Abilene Next Right," and then I was there, well into Tom Green County and to San Angelo.

The Butterfield Stage Line ran into the territory in 1858, south out of Fort Chadbourne, then west along the middle Concho toward Pecos and California, but Anglo settlers found no encouragement among Comanches, Apaches, and even Kickapoos until the army could get back to the frontier forts after the Civil War. Fort Concho was established in 1867, and that attracted settlers, among them Mr. B. J. Dewitt, who set up a trading post across the river from the fort. He named it Santa Angela after his wife's sister, a nun in Mexico, but an Anglo tongue turned it into San Angelo. The county was organized in 1874 and named for Thomas Green, a private in the Texas revolutionary army, a captain in the war with Mexico, and later a brigadier general in the Confederate Army before he was killed in 1864. Perhaps he should have refused the commission.

The highway into town took me directly onto the loop that circles the city. Down alongside San Angelo I turned right, or west, on the Paint Rock Road by the air force base. Soon Paint Rock Road turned into Avenue L, the fort off to my right, and I crossed South Bell, Christoval, the Concho River, South Oak, then South Chadbourne, Bryant, and went on, straight, to Monroe Street, and found Mindy and Bin and Andrew.

We visited quietly that afternoon and evening — Saturday. The next morning we went for late breakfast or early brunch at their favorite place, drove back to their home, and then it was time for me to go.

As I was leaving I told them what I had come to tell them, found no way except to blurt the news, that I was going to be married.

Sometimes, in arrogant — or solipsistic — splendor, I assume that what I plan to do is my business and none other's, and ineffably right. Mostly, however, as on that Sunday, I do not understand how I can be tolerated, let alone understood or forgiven. I do not understand. I think I shall never understand. But I did what I had come for — repudiated my life and, in my mind, theirs. They didn't take it that way, or seemed not to; seemed, rather, to reckon that I was at any rate theirs. I think I shall never understand.

And so I left; I eased down Monroe Street, turned onto Avenue L, crossed Bryant, South Chadbourne, South Oak, the Concho River, Christoval, South Bell, as Avenue L became the Paint Rock Road, came to the loop, turned, and headed back, on past the sign that said "Bronte Abilene Next Right" (you first go right, circle under a bridge, and then you're going left), past Red Creek and the sign that said "Tennyson 22," past Valentine Branch and Crownest Creek and Willow Creek and Mullins Cemetery and through Miles, past Little Concho Creek, through Rowena, to Ballinger, across the Colorado River.

Somewhere along there I began to feel almost all right, began to feel a little peaceful. Maybe it was because I thought I'd already done all the hurt I'd do that day, already shown the monstrous in myself, could now be a little easy. Maybe. Maybe it was because I didn't have to be embarrassed again that day, embarrassed to have them look at me. Maybe. Maybe I just felt better. Maybe. I drove on, past Long Branch and Bear Foot Creek and Butternut Creek and Mustang Creek and Middle Mustang and Mustang Creek again and Talpa. By this time I could see Santa Anna Peak ahead in the east, and I felt mostly good, mostly relaxed, mostly human, as if maybe I could go to a new life and be all right. It's going to be okay, I thought, and drove on past Home Creek and through Valera and past Mustang Branch and Wild Cat Creek. I drove through the deep cut in the rocky ridge and down the long slope. Just short of the bridge outside Santa Anna, the peak over me and ahead, I pulled over and stopped and got out, the peace that was not quite peace still on me; got out to stand, to drink coffee, and to look back at Mindy's gateway.

Back there, where I'd come from, was the long rise up to the cut I'd just come through. I thought I'd go on from where I'd come, thought, no, I can't leave Mindy's gateway, thought about which gates were open, guessed I knew which gates were closed, thought I'd come this far, thought I'd leave through Mindy's gate, go on.

I got back in the car, started it up, and looked to check the mirrors. The car was angled just so the side mirror framed it all perfectly. There it was, Mindy's gateway, the long rise up to the deep cut in the rocky ridge. Some gates open. Some gates close. None of them vanishes, even when you go on. They're there still, ahead, behind, in some mirror. I drove on.

Sources and Acknowledgments

2
The Search for the Perfect Peanut

I have mentioned a number of books and their authors here, and in some of these books I have worn the pages thin. Since I didn't quote directly from any of them, however, I thought that the identification given in the text would be sufficient.

3
After

I've depended on Jon Anderson's poem "In Sepia," from *The Milky Way: Poems 1967–1982* (New York: Ecco Press, 1983); Harold Bloom, *The Breaking of the Vessels* (Chicago: University of Chicago Press, 1982); Richard Lanham, *A Handlist of Rhetorical Terms* (Berkeley: University of California Press, 1968); and Jay Parini's poem "Things of This World," from *Town Life* (New York: Henry Holt, 1988).

Two works are quoted at greater length: lines from "Strange Lands," by Billy Collins, are reprinted by permission of the University of Arkansas Press from *The Apple That Astonished Paris*, copyright 1988 by Billy Collins; all of "Language Teaching: Naming," by Jenny Joseph, is reprinted by permission of Papier-Mache Press from *The Inland Sea*, copyright 1989 by Jenny Joseph.

4
Cast of Characters

I quote lines from Stephen Sandy's poem "The Sunday Outboard," in *Man in the Open Air* (New York: A.A. Knopf, 1988).

5
After

I quote lines from Denis Johnson's poem "The White Fires of Venus," in *The Incognito Lounge* (New York: Random House, 1982).

6
Which Text Do We Use in This Course?

I've depended on Denis Johnson again and on two poems by Wayne Dodd, "Before Divorce" and "November," from *Sometimes Music Rises* (Athens: University of Georgia Press, 1986). I've also cited Robert Pack, "Clayfield's Anniversary Song," from *Waking to My Name: New and Selected Poems* (Baltimore: Johns Hopkins University Press, 1980).

9
The Farm Is Gone

Here I've relied on John Graves, *Goodbye to a River* (New York: A. A. Knopf, 1961), and on Fred Chappell's poem "My Grandmother Washes Her Feet," from *River* (Baton Rouge: Louisiana State University Press, 1975).

15
Counting the Losses

I cite lines here from Mark Doty's poem "A Replica of the Parthenon," in *Turtle, Swan* (Boston: David Godine, 1987), and from Oscar Mandel's "Citizen Mandel, Ph.D.," in *Simplicities* (Los Angeles: Spectrum, 1974). I've also called on John Updike, "Seen the Film? Read the Book!" *New York Times*, June 28, 1987, section 2, pages 1 and 28, and on Eric Larsen, *An American Memory* (Chapel Hill: Algonquin Books, 1988). I quote at greater length from Raymond Carver: lines from "This Morning" are reprinted by permission of Tess Gallagher from *Ultramarine*, copyright Tess Gallagher.

17
The Snapshots I Have and the Snapshots I Don't Have

See Sharon Olds, "Little Things," from *The Gold Cell* (New York: A. A. Knopf, 1987); Larry McMurtry, *Leaving Cheyenne* (New York: Harper and Row, 1963); Gregory Orr, "Near Dawn," *We Must Make a Kingdom of It* (Middletown: Wesleyan University Press, 1986); and Jay Parini, "Town Life," from *Town Life*, already cited.

18
Already a Little Fuzzy Around the Edges

I've depended on Miller Williams's poem "Ruby Tells All," from *Imperfect Love* (Baton Rouge: Louisiana State University, 1986); Gregory Orr's "The Voyages," from *We Must Make a Kingdom of It*, already cited; Horst Kruger's *A Crack in the Wall* (New York: Fromm International Publishing Corporation, 1982); Pail Zweig's "The Hero in Literature," *Saturday Review*, December 1978; Max Apple's "Ripening Desire and the Muse of Middle Age," *New York Times Book Review*, March 1, 1987; Michael Wood's "Where the Wolf Howls," *New York Review of Books*, December 13, 1973; Harry Mulisch's "Death and the Maiden," *New York Review of Books*, July 17, 1986; Martin Gilbert's *The Holocaust: A History of the Jews in Europe during the Second World War* (New York: Holt, Rinehart and Winston, 1986); Gerald Stern's "I Do a Piece from Greece," from *Lovesick* (New York: Harper and Row, 1987); and John Ditsky's "Presence," from *Friend and Lover* (Princeton, N.J.: Ontario Review Press, 1981). I quote at greater length from Jack Myers: lines from "Do You Know What I Mean?" are reprinted by permission of Graywolf Press, Saint Paul, Minnesota, from *As Long as You're Happy*, copyright 1986 by Jack Myers.

19
Bob Coluci Died Last Week, and I'm Still Counting

Here I have used the following: Bharati Mukherjee, "Immigrant Writing: Give Us Your Maximalists," *New York Times Book Review*, August 28, 1988; Reynolds Price, "The Heroes of Our Times," *Saturday Review*, December 1978; Roger Shattuck, "Master Classes," *New York Review of Books*, April 19, 1979; Thomas Sanders, "Tribal Literature: Individual Identity and the Collective Unconscious," *College Composition and Communication*, October 1973; Keith McWalter, "Couch Dancing," *New York Times Magazine*, December 6, 1987; Langdon Gilkey, *Society and the Sacred* (New York: Crossroad, 1981); Ronald Schroeder, "Writing, Knowledge, and the Call for Objectivity," *College English*, February 1979; Kenneth Bruffee, "The Structure of Knowledge and the Future of Liberal Education," *Liberal Education*, Fall 1981; John Graves, *Goodbye to a River*, already cited; David H. Stewart, "The Decline of WASP Literature in America," *College English*, March 1969; Shirley Kaufman, "Wherever We're Not," in *Claims* (New York: Sheep Meadow Press, 1984); Ronald Reed, "To Discover Evil Is Easier Than to Comprehend It," *Fort Worth Star Telegram*, May 16, 1982; Lucy Dawidowicz, "Brothers, Write Down Everything," *New York Times Book Review*, February 25, 1979; Elie Wiesel, "Praising His Name in the Fire," *New York Times Book Review*, January 17, 1988; Horst Kruger, *A Crack in the Wall*, already cited; Gerald F. Linderman, *Embattled Courage: The Experience of Combat in the American Civil War* (New York: Free Press, 1987); Alistair Horne, *The Price of Glory* (New York: St. Martin's, 1962); C. K. Williams, "My Mother's Lips," in *Tar* (New York: Random House, 1980); Joyce Carol Oates, review of *Stories of Breece D'J Pancake*, *New York Times Book Review*, February 13, 1983; Alex Harris, ed., *A World Unsuspected* (Chapel Hill: University of North Carolina Press, 1987); and William Matthews, "Loyal," in *A Happy Childhood* (Boston: Little, Brown, 1984).

20

I Proposed a New Geography Course, but the Curriculum Committee Turned It Down

In this section, I depend on the following: Zulfikar Ghose, "It's Your Land, Boss," in *The Violent West* (New York: Macmillan, 1972); Sam Hamill, "A Lover's Quarrel," in *The Nootka Rose* (Portland, Oreg.: Breitenbush Books, 1987); Marilynne Robinson, "Writers and the Nostalgic Fallacy," *New York Times Book Review*, October 13, 1985; Earl Rovit, "In the Center Ring," *The American Scholar*, Winter 1969; Tom Asher, "Open Country," in *The Calling* (Cambridge, Mass.: alicejamesbooks, 1987); T. R. Hummer, "Cancer Rising," in *Lower-Class Heresy* (Urbana: University of Illinois Press, 1987); Frederick Turner, "Literature Lost in the Thickets," *New York Times Book Review*, February 15, 1987; Robin Doughty, "Wilderness or Garden? Conquering the Landscape," *Texas Humanist*, February 1985; Daniel J. Boorstein, *Hidden History* (New York: Harper and Row, 1987); Omar Bradley, *A Soldier's Story* (New York: Henry Holt, 1951); Larry L. King, "Requiem for a West Texas Town," *Harper's*, January 1966; Craig Clifford, *In the Deep Heart's Core* (College Station: Texas A&M University Press, 1985); Philip Roth, interview with Milan Kundera, *New York Times Book Review*, November 30, 1980.

Several sources I have relied on are identified in the text; I have not repeated them here.

I have quoted from two poems at greater length. T. R. Hummer's "The Rural Carrier Discovers That Love Is Everywhere" is reprinted by permission of the Louisiana State University Press from *The Angelic Orders*,

21

The Ache for Home

See Isaac Bashevis Singer, "Greenhorn in Seagate," *New York Times Magazine*, November 3, 1985; Reynolds Price, "Home: An American Obsession," *Saturday Review*, November 26, 1977; Psalm 103:15–16; Simone Weil, *The Need for Roots* (New York: Putnam, 1952); George Garrett, "Goodbye, Old Paint, I'm Leaving Cheyenne," in *For a Bitter Season* (Columbia: University of Missouri Press, 1967); Barney Nelson, *The Last Campfire: The Life Story of Ted Gray, a West Texas Rancher* (College Station: Texas A&M University Press, 1984); Douglas Southall Freeman, "The Last Parade," in Virginius Dabney, *The Last Review: The Confederate Reunion, Richmond, 1932* (Chapel Hill: Algonquin Books, 1984); Wendelgard von Staden, *Darkness over the Valley* (London: Ticknor and Fields, 1981); Horst Kruger, *A Crack in the Wall*, already cited; Louise Erdrich, "Where I Ought To Be," *New York Times Book Review*, July 28, 1985; Stephen Dobyns, "Querencia," in *Cemetery Nights*, already cited; "Five Ways to Wisdom," *Time*, September 27, 1982; Elizabeth Hardwick, "Seduction and Betrayal II," *New York Review of Books*, June 14, 1973; Michael Vincent Miller, "What Dracula Was Really Up To," *New York Times Book Review*, January 18, 1987; Lisel Mueller, "Midwestern Poetry: Goodbye to All That," in *In the Middle: Ten Midwestern Women Poets*, ed. Sylvia Griffith Wheeler (Kansas City, Kan.: BkMk Press, 1985); Robert Tyler, "History and the Ache of Time," *Forum*, Winter 1961–62; John Herbers, *The New Heartland: America's Flight Beyond the Suburbs and How It Is Changing Our Future* (New York: Times Book, 1986); Janice Doane and Devon Hodges, *Nostalgia and Sexual Difference* (New York and London: Methuen, 1987); Marilynne Robinson, "Writers and the Nostalgic Fallacy," already cited; and Frederick Garber, "Geographies and Languages and Selves and What They Do," *American Poetry Review*, September–October, 1985.

22
When Rhetorics Collide

See Michael Novak, "Television Shapes the Soul," in *Television as a Social Force* (New York: Praeger, 1975).

23
Speak, Memory

I have relied here on Mark Doty's "Paragon Park," from *Turtle, Swan*, already cited; Shirley Ann Grau, *Keepers of the House* (New York: A. A. Knopf, 1973); Loudon Wainwright's review of *A Good War*, by Studs Terkel, *New York Times Book Review*, October 7, 1984; Bruce Duffy, "The Do-It-Yourself Life of Ludwig Wittgenstein," *New York Times Book Review*, November 13, 1988; Dabney Stuart's poem, "Facing Up," in *Common Ground* (Baton Rouge: Louisiana State University Press, 1982); and Jeffrey Harrison's poem "Eminent Domain," in *The Singing Underneath* (New York: E. P. Dutton, 1988).

25
I Am the Twentieth Century

I have used the review by Jerome Bruner and Carol Fleisher Feldman of Nelson Goodman's *Of Mind and Other Matters* in the *New York Review of Books*, March 27, 1986.

26
The Lux Radio Theater

Here I've used the following: Molly Haskell, "Epic! Heroic! American!" *New York Times Book Review*, October 23, 1988; T. R. Hummer's poem, "Dogma: Pigmeat and Whiskey," from *Lower-Class Heresy*, already cited; Brooks Haxton's poem "Recess," from *Dominion* (New York: A. A. Knopf, 1986); Fred E. H. Schroeder, "And Now, a Word from the Silent Generation," *Western Humanities Review*, Winter 1969; Drew Middleton's review of Elmer Bendiner's *The Fall of Fortresses*, in *New York Times Book Review*, May 25, 1980; Edward Said, "Maestro for the Masses," *New York Times Book Review*, March 8, 1987; John Unruh, *The Plains Across* (Urbana: University of Illinois Press, 1979); Martin Middlebrook, *The Battle of Hamburg* (London: Allen Lane, 1980); Robert Craft, "Amorous in Amherst," *New York Review of Books*, April 23, 1987; Andrea Dworkin, *Intercourse* (New York: The Free Press, 1987); Marilyn Coffey, "The Dust Storms," *Natural History*, February, 1978; and A. C. Greene, "God in West Texas," *Arlington Quarterly* Autumn 1967.

I have quoted at greater length from three poems. Joan Joffe Hall's "Romance and Capitalism at the Movies" is reprinted by permission of alicejamesbooks from *Romance and Capitalism at the Movies*, copyright by Joan Joffe Hall. Lines from Sylvia Moss's "Green Fields of France" are reprinted by permission of the author and the University of Illinois Press from *Cities in Motion*, copyright 1987 by Sylvia Moss. Joseph Colin Murphey's "Panhandle Piety" is reprinted by permission of Prickly Pear Press from *A Return to the Landscape*, copyright 1979 by Joseph Colin Murphey.

28
Domestic Privacies

I've relied on Herbert Gold's review of *My Mother's Sabbath Days*, by Chaim Grade, in the *New York Times Book Review*, November 16, 1986; Jay Parini's "Town Life," already cited; Mark Doty's "Rocket," in *Turtle, Swan*, already cited; Francine Prose, *Household Saints* (New York: St. Martin's, 1981); and Miller Williams, "In Nashville, Standing on the Wooden Circle Sawed Out from the Old Ryman Stage, the Picker Has a Vision," from *The Boys on Their Bony Mules* (Baton Rouge: Louisiana State University Press, 1983).

31
To the Jayton Cemetery

I've used David Bottoms's poem "In a U-Haul North of Damascus," from *The Made Thing*, ed. Leon Stokesbury (Fayetteville: University of Arkansas Press, 1987).